D1085690

Truths
that Make
a Difference

Lavonn D. Brown

TRUTHS
THAT MAKE
A DIFFERENCE

Lavonn D. Brown

compiled by Martha Jo Glazner

CONVENTION PRESS
Nashville, Tennessee

This book is the text for Youth Course 3376
in the Subject Area of Baptist Doctrine of the
Church Study Course.

Dewey Decimal Classification Number: 230.6

Printed in the United States of America
This book has been adapted from *I Believe* and *I Believe, Volume 2*.

Editing Staff
Martha Jo Glazner
Editor/Design Editor
Ruby L. McMillin
Assistant Editor
R. Clyde Hall, Jr.
Supervisor, Youth Section
Nolan P. Howington
Curriculum Coordinator
Roy T. Edgemon
Director, Church Training Department
Design Staff
Marion M. Farrar
Artist-Designer
Robert L. Seale
Art Supervisor
Photographer
Nancy Robinson

Other Youth Section Personnel
Charles Doggett
Editor
Larry Garner
Editor
Bettina G. Terry
Assistant Editor
Joyce Frazier
Ginny Bollinger
Manuscript Assistants
Wayne Jenkins
Consultant
J. Larry Yarborough
Youth Specialist
Christian Development Division
Howard B. Foshee
Director

Contents

The Writer—Lavonn D. Brown

This book has many sources, but the primary source is the mind and heart of Lavonn D. Brown. The seedbed was the youth discussion group at First Baptist Church, Norman, Oklahoma, where he is pastor. To form the framework of the book, Dr. Brown used questions youth asked about basic Baptist doctrines. Printed first as *I Believe* and *I Believe, Volume 2*, this book gives unity to doctrinal study and provides an overview of major Baptist beliefs.

Brown, a well-known Southern Baptist pastor, speaker, and leader, has served as president of the Oklahoma Baptist Convention. He and his wife Norma Lee, a talented artist, have three sons—Bob, Scott, and Nathan.

Introduction

The symbol of our age is the question mark. If you could open the skull of an average American, you might find a coin purse, a degree from a university, and a bundle of question marks.

This book is a sincere effort to answer questions many people *are* asking about some "truths that make a difference." Many of the insights of this book and the questions raised were first discussed with young people.

Interrobang⁈

Interrobang is a cross between the question mark and the exclamation point. It is the symbol for paradox, though a paradox is generally more serious. *Interrobang* is used in a semi-humorous context. It admits that you can affirm some things while you wrestle with others. You don't have to know everything to affirm some things. Interrobang is a fitting symbol for this book.

This book makes no claim to answer all the questions people are asking about our Baptist doctrines. It does present some truths, however, which individuals may affirm while they work out their questions in other areas. For the purposes of this study, *interrobang* will be used to describe what must have been in the mind of the man who brought his son to Jesus for healing: "Lord, I believe; help thou mine unbelief" (Mark 9:24). Affirmation is followed by question.

Interrobang⁈

The purpose of this book is to present a doctrinal study on some carefully selected subjects—truths that make a difference. Many things are true but do not make a difference. Countless ideas that are true may not be worth your attention, much less your life. For instance, I remember hearing that the average manhole cover weighs eighty-eight pounds. That may be true, but I'm not willing to die for it.

What is "doctrine"? "Rules," you answer. But, you are wrong. The word simply means teaching or instruction. It merely implies the acceptance of a principle as taught by a body of believers. So, when we speak of the "doctrine of God," we are merely referring to those teachings about God which are commonly accepted by Baptists.

I remember one young person asking, "Who 'makes up' the Baptist beliefs?" Any answer must begin, *"No one person."* In this respect, Baptists are an amazing people. No one person would ever attempt to write an official statement of Baptist beliefs. The materials projected in this book are the efforts of one Southern Baptist. It is hoped that the final product will be in agreement with the faith and message of Baptists everywhere.

These materials are presented with a prayer that people will be helped and encouraged in their search for truth. Some people may feel that they are overexposed to truth. Nevertheless, truth should never be feared. Nor should it be rejected as truth merely because of its source.

Are you ready for the search into "truths that make a difference"? If so, begin with a Bible nearby. Pray for the guidance of the Holy Spirit as you seek to discover God's truths.

CHAPTER 1

What Is God Like?

Memory Verses: *John 4:24; 1 John 1:5; 1 John 4:8*

Let's begin our search for truth with a study of the nature

of $\dfrac{\theta\epsilon\acute{o}s}{\textbf{God}}$ The symbol of our search will be a circle for

infinity: without beginning ◯ without end.

It is never easy to put our faith into words. And, then, about the time we have said it we receive new insights. Our faith is never a final faith. We can never put it away for safekeeping.

So, let me affirm one of the basic elements of my faith. I BE-LIEVE IN GOD. For me, this is a *truth that makes a difference*. I do not understand everything there is to know about God, but that does not disturb me.

INTERROBANG ‽ Remember, it is possible to affirm our belief in God while we continue our search for greater understanding.

So, you believe in God? Big deal! The questions is, What kind of God do you believe in? Do you believe that man has been created in the image of God or that God has been created in the image of man? Do you believe that God's nature is such that he created man for fellowship or that man's nature is such that he "projected" God for his own comfort?

Before you read this chapter, take a minute to write down your ideas about God. What does the word *God* mean to you? What do you visualize, if anything? At this moment, what is God like to you?

_____

_____

What God *Is Not* Like

Many people wrestle with concepts of God that are totally inadequate. J. B. Phillips wrote a book entitled *Your God Is Too Small.* It is his feeling that many people are living with inner dissatisfaction or without any faith simply because their God is not big enough.

How can we trust our lives to a God who is absent, distant, impersonal, remote, standing in the shadows or staying at a safe distance? Maturing young people find it difficult to give their adult loyalties to a childish concept of God.

Many people often get hung up on a concept of God which is totally inadequate. They are like the schoolboy who was asked what he thought God was like. He answered, "The sort of person who is always snooping around to see if anyone is having a good time and trying to stop it."

For this boy, God is much like the "Resident Policeman" concept of J. B. Phillips. In such a case it is difficult to distinguish between God and the "still small voice" of human conscience. God becomes a cosmic killjoy whose greatest pleasure is in keeping us from having a good time. Is this your concept of God? If so, you have an unsatisfactory God.

Many psychologists remind us that our early concept of God is closely related to our idea of father. Phillips has called this a "parental hangover." Perhaps this is a natural stage in the process of a maturing faith. A concept of God that is based primarily on fear, however, will never provide a satisfactory foundation for adult Christianity.

Other people view God as a "Grand Old Man," who "was a great power in His day, but could not possibly be expected to keep pace with modern progress!"[1] To some people, God is an old gentleman with a long beard and gray hair. He sits on a great, ornate throne "up there" gazing down at the world of men. This concept of God as old (and consequently old-fashioned) is inadequate for today's people.

Another problem develops when we picture God as a mere magnified human being—a giant man. In this case, God becomes a "Managing Director," responsible for the successful operation of a vast universe. He cannot be expected to take detailed interest in a single human life. When we think of God in such human terms, he becomes little more than a frustrated telephone operator sitting at a giant switchboard, busily plugging in on poor mortals. Remember, it is man who is made in the image of God and not God made in the image of man.

The author is not implying that the above concepts of God are false. The point is that they are inadequate. In some of these instances God is "too small." In others, God is "too big."

Will the Real God Please Stand?

Is it possible for us to know the real God? Yes, it is possible. Most of us have to work our way around some inadequate concepts in coming to know the real God. That's no problem as long as we do not get discouraged and quit.

How is it possible to know the real God? God is more interested in being known than we are in knowing him. God has made himself known in many ways. He speaks through many voices. He has left us with many sources of knowledge concerning himself. When Paul and Barnabas attempted to tell the Gentiles at Lystra about the living God, they said, "But he has always given evidence of his existence by the good things he does: he gives you rain from heaven and crops at the right times; he gives you food and fills your hearts with happiness" (Acts 14:17, GNB).[2]

As I think back over my own experience, I discover that God made himself known to me in various ways. God kept breaking into my world of awareness even though my home would probably fall under the category of "nominally Christian." If you would permit me a personal testimony, I would like to tell you how I came to believe in God or how God revealed himself to me.

1. *God made himself known to me in his people.* My earliest impressions of God came by observation. My mother was a praying and compassionate woman. My father, though not a Christian at the time, made it possible for me to believe in a God who loves, cares, and provides for his own. My heritage was enriched by devout, churchgoing grandparents. Christian homes, churchgoing young

people, worn Bibles, churches, and Christian art all spoke to me of God.

God had his "living letters," and I read every one of them. These were human letters "written not with ink, but with the Spirit of the living God, not on tablets of stone, but on tablets of human hearts" (2 Cor. 3:3, NASB).[3] Some of these letters were confusing to me, as I know they must be to you. Others were unmistakably clear. These bothered me. They reminded me of a God I was trying to forget.

I watched God at work in his people, producing the fruits of the Spirit—gentleness, kindness, and thoughtfulness. In fact, God was producing in them those virtues that were noticeably absent in my own life. I was never able to discard what God was so obviously accomplishing in the lives of his people.

When all other evidence failed, there remained one evidence that was impossible to ignore: the changes God brought about in human nature.

2. *My next impression of God came from that which he had created.* For me, God became increasingly necessary to explain an ordered universe and man's moral consciousness.

God began to speak a new language. When I looked into the microscope and telescope, God spoke the language of beauty, order, harmony, balance, design, and predictability. The heavens began telling of the glory of God. The earth "is declaring the work of His hands" (Ps. 19:1, NASB).

The "image of God" in man was never difficult for me to accept or believe. Man's capacity to initiate, achieve, do, and finish, all revealed divine imprint. I was never able to accept casually man's intelligence, sense of right and wrong, and universal consciousness of divine presence. All these spoke to me of God.

I realize that neither design in nature nor mankind's moral capacity can prove God to one who chooses not to believe. Even though these experiences were not conclusive, they were powerful. I could not ignore them altogether.

3. *Then, God began to make himself known to me through the Bible—his written Word.* When I was in high school, for reasons unknown to me, I began reading the Bible. I discovered an old, half-burned Bible in the projection room of the local theatre where

I worked. During the brief intervals between the reels of film, I read the Bible. As I read the thrilling stories, it slowly dawned on me that these were real people in a real world who had undergone real experiences with a real God.

God began to speak a new language. His approach at this time was more direct, more personal. At the same time, there seemed to be a maturing in my own receptiveness to God's attempt to reveal himself.

The Scriptures began to have a "ring of truth" about them. There was something within me which reached out in highest hope toward the one beginning to reveal himself. The Bible took on the characteristics of authority, sufficiency, and certainty. No one had told me that "All Scripture is inspired by God" (2 Tim. 3:16, GNB).

I discovered that the Bible called for a life-style and a type of moral character which would be more acceptable to God. I fell far short of the expected quality of life. In fact, I doubted if I would even register on the scales. If someone had asked me, "Do you understand what you are reading?" my answer would have been, "How can I unless someone helps me?" At this point no one had told me, "These have been written in order that you may believe that Jesus is the Messiah, the Son of God, and that through your faith in him you may have life" (John 20:31, GNB).

4. *Finally, God made himself known to me in his Son—Jesus Christ.* I do not know exactly when the awareness came. As I read the life of Christ in the Gospels, I slowly began to realize that in him we see what God must be like. Even the early disciples looked at Jesus and saw something eternally true about God.

What is God like? Paul wrote: "God was in Christ reconciling the world to Himself" (2 Cor. 5:19, NASB). The writer of Hebrews, after showing that God had spoken in many different ways through the ages, concluded, "But in these last days he has spoken to us through his Son" (Heb. 1:2, GNB). John wrote, "No one has ever seen God. The only Son, . . . has made him known" (John 1:18, GNB).

God had unmistakably made himself known to me. At the time, I could have given you many reasons why I didn't want to become a Christian. But, God kept breaking into my world. I could no longer plead ignorance of God—only indifference. I knew I could not go on ignoring him indefinitely. I realized that the life I was living would not do. So, I listened with new ears to his soft, but insistent, voice as he spoke to me concerning the emptiness and meaninglessness of my life. He promised that a new life was awaiting me. I searched. I believed. I followed. Only then did the Holy Spirit move in with the assurance, certainty, and presence of God that I so desired.

God Is Spirit

John must be considered as a respected theologian. In his effort to help us understand what God is like, he said, "God is a Spirit" (John 4:24); "God is light" (1 John 1:5); and "God is love" (1 John 4:8). Although these three statements affirm some things about God which are eternally true, they also rule out many false concepts about him.

First, John has affirmed that *God is a spirit*. As such he is present in the first chapter of the Bible, "the Spirit of God was moving over the face of the deep" (Gen. 1:2, RSV),[6] and in the last chapter of the Bible, " 'The Spirit and the bride say, "Come" ' " (Rev. 22:17, RSV). All in between is God's revelation and man's discovery of God as spirit.

Before John's affirmation can be fully understood, we will need to investigate carefully the occasion. It took place at a time when Jesus felt that he "must needs" go through Samaria. Why did he feel this moral necessity? His disciples would certainly discourage going into Samaritan territory. After all, the Jews had no dealings with the Samaritans. It was customary for Jews traveling north to cross the Jordan and go up on the Eastern side to avoid deliberately the land of Samaria. Yet, Jesus felt necessity for going that way. Why? Let's see.

About noon they arrived at the small village of Sychar and came to Jacob's well. The long walk and hot sun had taken their toll. Jesus was tired and sat down at the well for a period of rest. The disciples went into Sychar to buy food.

While Jesus sat alone at the well, a woman came to draw water. We learn later that she was a woman of poor character and bad reputation. Jesus knew all that. It is always a surprise—though it shouldn't be—to discover that Jesus often spoke some of his most remarkable words to the least remarkable people.

For a starter, Jesus asked the woman for a drink of water. The woman's response was typical. It was a conditioned response, learned through many years of prejudice. "Are you a stranger in these parts? Why would *you*, since you are a Jew, ask for a drink from *me*, a 'despised Samaritan'? Don't you know that Jews don't speak to Samaritans?"

Jesus understood the woman's feelings and responded with a gentle reminder, "If you only knew what a wonderful gift God has for you, and who I am, you would ask me for some *living* water" (John 4:10, TLB).[4] Jesus proceeded to tell her about the water that does not come from Jacob's well; water that becomes a perpetual spring within, springing up into eternal life.

In the course of the conversation, the words of Jesus began to get too close to home. The woman responded with one of mankind's favorite diversionary tactics, "What is the true church?" She asked, "Where should we worship, in Jerusalem or here at Mount Gerizim?"

Jesus responded with the remarkable words that contain the affirmation, "God is Spirit." He replied, "God is Spirit, and only by the power of his Spirit can people worship him as he really is" (John 4:24, GNB).

What do you think John was trying to tell us about God when he said, "God is Spirit"? Before you go on, take a minute to write down what "God is Spirit" means to you now. _____

_____

_____

_____

Perhaps it would be good to begin by discovering what is ruled out by this important concept. If God is spirit, then some of our false and inadequate concepts of God are ruled out. For instance, many people appear to worship a God who was created in the image of man. If God is spirit, the idea that God is simply a projection of our childish desire for a loving heavenly Father is ruled out. The idea that God has a body with feet, arms, hands, eyes, ears, and a mouth like man's is also ruled out. If God is spirit, we must eliminate the idea that God must think as we think, have the same human characteristics we have, and be automatically opposed to the same things we are. We must confess that his ways are above our ways, and his thoughts are above our thoughts.

Other people consider religious faith as a form of psychological "escapism." They feel that those who place faith in God are attempting to escape from the realities of life. If God is spirit, however, we must rule out the concept that God is "a heavenly bosom" out there somewhere to which men fly to escape.

Now, let's consider what is affirmed by this concept. If God is spirit . . . then what? What does this tell us about the nature of God, and what can we expect from him?

In the first place, we know that God is invisible. He cannot be seen by the human eye. John asserted, "No one has ever seen God" (John 1:18, GNB). The Colossian letter speaks of the invisible or unseen God. (See Col. 1:15.) This idea seems simple enough. Yet, it is one of the most difficult ideas for us to accept. The history of idolatry is the history of man attempting to make a God that he can see. Man has always desired to ascribe form, location, space, and time to God. This problem is in the background of the First Commandment: "Worship no god but me. Do not make for yourselves images of anything. . . . for I am the Lord your God" (Deut. 5:7-10, GNB).

The second truth we know about the nature of God is that *he is present everywhere* and, therefore, can be worshiped anywhere. Jesus told the woman of a time when men will not worship God on Mount Gerizim or in Jerusalem (John 4:21). God is not confined to places. He is not restricted by time and space. He cannot be confined to mountaintops nor enclosed by church walls. (See Ps. 139:7-12).

Because God is spirit and, therefore, present everywhere, we may affirm a third great truth: *God is always near and approachable.* He is personally present with every believer. John has affirmed, "No one has ever seen God, but if we love one another, God lives in union with us, and his love is made perfect in us" (1 John 4:12, GNB).

Because God is spirit, we must be genuine and sincere in our worship. Jesus said that we must worship him in spirit and in truth. This would be the very opposite of pretense and superficiality. We must think God to be naïve to imagine that he does not see through our pretense, shallowness, and unworthy motives.

God Is Light

Theologians have spoken of God's steadfastness, knowledge, sovereignty, and powerfulness. But, John, the beloved disciple, simply declared that God is spirit, light, and love.

John's second affirmation is that "God is light." As such, he is present in the first chapter of the Bible (TLB): "Then God said, 'Let there be light'; and there was light. And God saw that the light was good; and God separated the light from the darkness" (Gen. 1:3-4, NASB). In the last chapter of the Bible we read, "And there shall be no night there; and they will need no candle, neither light of the sun; for the Lord God giveth them light: and they shall reign for ever and ever" (Rev. 22:5). And, all in between, there runs a continual contrast between light and darkness.

People speak a universal language that says we love light and we fear darkness. Light stands for life, truth, reality, holiness, and glory. Darkness stands for ignorance, sin, nothingness, moral blindness, and death. It is little wonder that John affirmed, "God is light." Physically, light represents glory; intellectually, it represents truth; morally, it represents holiness.

This insight into God's nature was not exactly new with John. In the Old Testament there are references to God as light. The psalmist declared, "The Lord is my light and my salvation; whom shall I fear?" (Ps. 27:1). The prophet, Isaiah, wrote, "The Lord will be your everlasting light, and your God will be your glory" (Isa. 60:19, RSV). The theme of light also became a key to understanding messianic prophecy: "The people who walk in darkness shall see a great Light—a Light that will shine on all those who live in the land of the shadow of death" (Isa. 9:2, TLB).

The New Testament references to light and darkness are less frequent but have fuller meaning. John's own usage of this theme is progressive and advanced. In the prologue of John's gospel, he made it clear that the light Jesus brings will overcome the world's darkness. "Eternal life is in him, and this life gives light to all mankind. His life is the light that shines through the darkness—and the darkness can never extinguish it" (John 1:4-5, TLB). The light

There is not enough darkness in all the world to put out one lighted candle.

Jesus brings to man has an unconquerable quality. When his light comes, the darkness is dispelled, but his light is not defiled. The light of Christ puts to flight man's oldest fear—the fear of darkness.

The light Christ brings shows things exactly as they are. That light strips away disguises, masks, and outer wrappings. In the beginning of his public ministry Jesus said to Nicodemus: "The light is come into the world, and men loved the darkness rather than the light; for their deeds were evil. For everyone who does evil hates the light, and does not come to the light, lest his deeds should be exposed" (John 3:19-20, NASB). Paul said, "For light is capable of 'showing up' everything for what it really is" (Eph. 5:13, Phillips).[5] This is the last thing most of us would like to have happen.

On two different occasions Jesus declared, "I am the light of the world" (John 8:12; 9:5). This is a claim Jesus made concerning himself: therefore, it gives us insight into the nature and character of God. The first occasion was during the Feast of Tabernacles. On the first evening the people gathered in the Temple treasury for the ceremony called the illumination of the Temple. When the four great candelabra were set ablaze, their light extended throughout Jerusalem. Jesus said: "I am the light of the world. . . . Whoever follows me will have the light of life and will never walk in darkness" (John 8:12). The second occasion was after Jesus had restored the sight of the man born blind. (Read John 9:5.) It is amazing that anyone could actually prefer darkness when Christ himself is the Light of the world.

The light of Christ is intended to dispel the world's darkness. The followers of Christ are to share this responsibility as they become reflectors of that light. "You are the world's light . . . glowing in the night for all to see. . . . Let it shine for all" (Matt. 5:14-15, TLB). Just as the moon, dark and sterile in itself, reflects the light of the sun, each follower of Christ is to reflect his heavenly light into the world's darkness.

Finally, John affirmed that "God is light and in him is no darkness at all" (1 John 1:5-7, RSV). John was trying to get us better acquainted with the real God. What does this great affirmation tell us about God? First of all, it tells us that God wishes to be known. Light is self-revealing. There is nothing secretive or concealed about God. The affirmation also speaks of the purity and holiness of God. Light is the complete opposite of everything evil and dark. For that reason, the light of the gospel creates an immediate consciousness of sin. It requires open honesty with God at the point of the basic wrongness, purposelessness, and meaninglessness of our lives. Then, the concept of God as light speaks of God's interest in giving guidance for our lives. His light makes our path clear. Our future paths are gradually illuminated as his light shines "more and more." His word becomes a lamp to our feet and a light to our paths. Our responsibility is to walk in that light.

God Is Love

Now we come to some of the greatest words ever spoken. These words are well worth all the languages ever written, studied, or spoken. What is God like? "God is love" (1 John 4:8). Undoubtedly this is the most beautiful and profound passage in the letter.

Read slowly 1 John 4:7-21 in *The Good News Bible.* Imagine that you are reading these verses *for the very first time.* You have never seen a Bible before!

First John 4:7-21 contains John's outstanding contribution to Christian theology. He made a profound contribution to our understanding of both divine and human love. Perhaps the following diagram will give you a summary of love's relationships explored by John.

God is the source of love: "Love is of God" (1 John 4:7).

MAN'S LOVE FOR MAN

"If God so loved us, we ought also to love one another" (1 John 4:11).

GOD'S LOVE TO MAN (John 3:16)

MAN'S LOVE FOR GOD "We love him, because he first loved us" (1 John 4:19).

God is the source of love. John was careful to point out that love comes from God (1 John 4:7). Our ability to love is merely a reflection of divine love. We are never closer to God or nearer what we were meant to be than when we love.

As the source of love, God is actively expressing this love for man. He expresses his love so much that John felt love is the most accurate description of what God is like: "God is love." When you consider God's attributes, love would be closely related to all of them.

20

Is it too much to hope that God's love is constant? Many people are exposed to a kind of parental love that is conditional. Love is shown only when certain conditions are met. "Do this; don't do that; and I will love you." When these conditions are not met, love is withdrawn. God's love is not optional or conditional; it is constant.

In fact, it is by love that God is best known and most often discovered. We see the effect of his love at work in the lives of his people. No man has ever seen the wind; only the effect of the wind is seen. No one has ever seen God; only the effect of his love is seen.

Maybe you have questions.

- If God is a God of love, why is the world in the mess it's in?
- How can God love someone like me?
- Why does he allow evil?
- Does God *really* have a plan for *my* particular life, and is it possible that I can be someone of worth in God's eyes and in people's eyes?

These questions find their partial answer, at least, in the fact that God is love. He created us with free will and choice, because he wanted our love to be free and spontaneous. Otherwise, he would have made robots or puppets. In *The Gospel of John* by William Barclay we have been reminded that love is not love unless man is free not to love. God went to the trouble to redeem us, because a God of love must seek and save the lost. He gives us eternal life, because a God of love desires to have continual, eternal fellowship with the man created in his image.

The greatest demonstration of God's love is in the gift of his Son. "God showed his love for us by sending his only Son into the world so that we might have life through him. This is what love is" (1 John 4:9-10, GNB). Without the life, love, and death of Christ, John could never have said, "God is love." If you want to believe that God is love, then study the life of Christ, keeping in mind that he said, "He who has seen me has seen the Father" (John 14:9, RSV).

We also have the ability to love. We are created in the image of a God of love. God's love is given in anticipation of our returned love. John affirmed that human love is a response to revealed divine love. This human love should express itself in two directions:

in love for God and in love for one another.

God loved first, and our love is in response to his love. (See 1 John 4:19.) Our ability to love is not merely the product of human love: it is a gift from God.

This love for God will also issue in love for one another. In John's mind, love for God and love for others were inseparable. (Read 1 John 4:11.) The only way to prove our love for God is to love the people God loves. John showed how difficult (if not im-

possible) it is for love and hate to abide in the same heart. "If someone says he loves God, but hates his brother, he is a liar. For he cannot love God, whom he has not seen, if he does not love his brother, whom he has seen" (1 John 4:20, GNB).

An American journalist in China watched a missionary nurse cleaning the sores of wounded soldiers in a hospital. "I wouldn't do that for a million dollars," the visitor said.

Without pausing in her work, the nurse quietly replied, "Neither would I." And such is love.

Interrobang? It is possible to affirm some things while we continue the search. It is my firm conviction that no one has been left completely alone by God. My prayer is that you can now affirm, "I BELIEVE IN GOD."

Why are you not actively seeking God? Could it be that you fear the changes he would want to make in your life? In the book *Mere Christianity*, C. S. Lewis told what he often did as a child when a toothache developed. He knew if he went to his mother, she would give him something to deaden the pain and make it possible for him to sleep. He knew something else. She would take him to the dentist the next morning. The dentist would not be content to relieve the pain. He would want to set all his teeth permanently right. So, the lad determined to bear the pain as long as possible.

Many people avoid going to God for the same reason. They would like to be cured of one particular sin, but they know God will not stop there. Once you call him in, he will give you the full treatment. If he is spirit, light, and love, however, you could be in no safer, more sympathetic hands.

Honestly Now

Write a letter to God. This letter is not to be shared with anyone. Name the three most important things in your life. Tell God how much you need his love and how you love him. End your letter with this thought: "I am a person of worth because I have been created in the image of God. God is love."

CHAPTER 2

When God Became Flesh

Memory Verses: *Matthew 16:16; John 1:14* (cards 4-5)

The next area of our search for truth will involve us in a study of

the nature of $\underline{\quad \chi\rho\iota\sigma\tau\acute{o}s \quad}$
Christ

The symbol of our search will be the fish,

one of the early symbols for Christianity. The reason is simple. The Greek word for fish formed an acrostic with special meaning:

I = Jesus
X = Christ
Θ = God
Υ = Son
Σ = Savior

In each case the Greek letter is the first letter in the Greek word for five names. Altogether the acrostic reads, "Jesus Christ, Son of God, Savior." Early followers of Christ, under constant threat of persecution, used the sign of the fish to let others know they were Christians.

The previous chapter stated that God desired to be known by man. God has made himself known in many ways and through many witnesses. The most personal and unmistakable revelation of God was in his Son—Jesus Christ.

I BELIEVE IN CHRIST. I also believe that, in Jesus Christ, God has come to man. This is a *truth that has made a difference* in my life. I do not understand everything there is to know about the divine-human Christ. Yet, I am not disturbed. It is a confession of faith that I am constrained and bound to make.

INTERROBANG **?** Remember, it is possible to affirm our belief in Christ while we continue our search for a greater understanding of "God in the flesh."

So you believe in Christ? Tremendous! The question is, Who is Jesus Christ? The answer to that question will determine whether this is a truth that makes a difference.

Before proceeding, write one brief sentence stating your concept

of Christ. Who is he? What is your opinion of him? _____

_____

_____

Inadequate Concepts of Christ

Many people live with totally inadequate concepts of Christ. Their indifference to Christ is the only evidence needed. No one can come to a knowledge of Christ as Son of God and remain indifferent.

Christians and non-Christians alike agree that Christ was the greatest man who ever lived. But is that all we can say?

"I feel that Jesus was a great man," said one young person. "He had great insight and empathy, but he was just a great prophet, not the Son of God." Most people are willing to add the name of Jesus to their long list of the greatest men who ever lived.

Many non-Christians look upon Jesus as a great human teacher. They are deeply impressed by his wisdom and insight. Even people of other religions praise him for his great system of ethics. Some people follow him because he heads their list as the Master Teacher. But is that the final truth? Can nothing more be said?

For the disciples of Jesus, it was exam day. Jesus needed a clear-cut confession from his followers as to who he was. Popular opinions were varied and divided.

The place was Caesarea Philippi. Storm clouds were gathering. Jesus had sought this opportunity to be alone with his disciples. He knew the end was near. Had anyone recognized him for who and what he was? Would there be anyone to carry on his work? The survival of his mission was at stake.

Jesus began his challenge with an easy question, "Who are the people saying that I am?" The disciples felt safe and comfortable with this question, because popular opinions were numerous.

They replied, "Some say John the Baptist; some, Elijah; and others, Jeremiah, or one of the other prophets" (Matt. 16:14, NASB).

Opinions were unanimous that Jesus was someone great. He was considered the reincarnation of one of the greatest prophets. Surely Jesus would be satisfied to be classified in such great company.

The wise examiner moved gently from the simple to the difficult, from the impersonal to the personal. He asked them, "Who do *you* say that I am?" (Matt. 16:15, NASB). This was the question of all questions. The answer did not come so easily, but Simon did not disappoint his Lord. Are you ready for his answer?

"You are, 'The Messiah, the Son of the living God'" (Matt. 16:16, GNB).

Essentially, Peter had discovered that no human categories, descriptions, or classifications were adequate to describe Jesus Christ. Jesus was more than a great man, teacher, or prophet. This conviction came by living in the company and presence of Jesus. After Simon's great and noble confession, Jesus knew his work was in safe hands.

Will the Real Jesus Please Stand?

Almost two thousand years ago, in Galilee, there lived a man who knew God. His name was Jesus. He came to be known as the Christ—the Anointed One. His name is familiar to nearly everyone. But is it possible to know his name and the man himself remain a mystery?

A number of years ago I knew a lovely young girl named Norma Lee. At first I was content to know her name. As we became better acquainted, I was more interested in knowing the person behind the name. Our relationship matured to the point that I asked her to marry me. After more than twenty years of marriage, the name is still precious. But, I have come to love, appreciate, and respond to the person behind the name. Many people know her by name. I know her as a person of worth who brings out the best in me.

It is possible for individuals to grow up in a Christian home,

26

"For two thousand years Jesus Christ has been the one central character of human history."[1]

Anonymous

faithfully attend a Christian church, study the Bible in Sunday School, and still know little about Jesus Christ as a person. Coming to know a person requires a commitment similar to marriage. In that continual commitment we come to love, appreciate, and respond to the person who bears the name.

The real Jesus is worth knowing. He has continued to haunt the thinking and conscience of all men. In Jesus, God has come to us.

27

At this one definite point the living God has broken through into history. Our familiarity with his coming has dulled its wonder for us.

Our family loves to spend some time each summer in the Colorado mountains. I always enjoy coming to a high mountain pass where the water courses divide and flow in separate directions. Even though I have seen it many times, the wonder remains. Raindrops falling on one side of the Continental Divide flow eastward and ultimately wind their way toward the Atlantic. Only a few yards away raindrops form a tiny stream to begin a long winding journey westward toward the Pacific. I experience a reverence to know I am standing at the watershed, where all the streams divide.

Jesus Christ has split history in much the same way. Every event in human history is now dated with reference to his coming. History is divided into two eras—B.C. (Before Christ) and A.D. (*anno Domini*, Latin for "In the Year of Our Lord"). Any person who has so influenced human history is worth our knowing.

Then God Became Flesh

God made man in his image. God took a calculated risk when he made man free. God desired to love and be loved. He made us with free will and choice, because he wanted our love to be free and spontaneous.

In exercising his free will, man chose the way of sin and rebellion. The results: Man was separated from the God of love, severed from his own better self, and isolated from perfect fellowship with other men.

God was faced with a challenging problem. On one hand was sinful man living in deliberate rebellion. On the other hand was a holy God who must be both loving and just. How could the holy God and the sinful man be brought together? God could not condemn all mankind because that would be inconsistent with love. He could not save all mankind indiscriminately because that would be inconsistent with justice.

One other alternative was open to God. He could send a mediator who would pay the price God himself demanded, leaving the decision with men of free will. John described this alternative when he said, "Before anything else existed, there was Christ, [the Word] with God. He has always been alive and is himself God. . . . And Christ became a human being and lived here on earth among us and was full of loving forgiveness and truth" (John 1:1,14, TLB). At one point in history God became flesh and lived among men.

We call God's carefully chosen alternative the *incarnation*. The name is derived from the Latin words *in carnis* meaning "in the flesh." What the incarnation actually affirms is that the man Jesus of Nazareth was in a unique sense the self-expression of God.

The word *incarnation* does not appear in the Bible, but the idea does: "For in Christ there is all of God in a human body" (Col. 2:9, TLB). And Paul wrote, "For God was in Christ, restoring the world to himself" (2 Cor. 5:19, TLB). In the incarnation we are confronted with a great miracle: That God would manifest himself in a flesh and blood body. We are also confronted with a great mystery that is beyond human understanding.

The INTERROBANG is a fitting symbol for the incarnation— when God became flesh. The doctrine of incarnation is an expression of the Christian conviction that Jesus was truly man, and at the same time, truly God.

Was Jesus Fully Human?

Christians have always had difficulty realizing that Jesus was fully, completely, and truly human. It is easier to think of him as God in human disguise.

The first heresy ever condemned by the early church was a denial of the true manhood of Jesus. For two thousand years devoted Christians have tended to depict Jesus as a divine being who merely *seemed* to be human.

Read the Gospel accounts again. The dominant fact which stands out is that Jesus was a man—an extraordinary man to be sure, but nonetheless a man.

His birth was a *human birth*. We often lose sight of the humanity of his birth because of the star, the angelic announcements, the heavenly choirs, and the Wise Men. It is difficult to concentrate on the human aspects when the sky was punctured by voices and heaven was leaking through to earth. But let's try.

Mary was a human mother. She should be neither worshiped nor ignored. Scholars and historians insist that she was a young woman. Because she shared the fallen nature common to all mankind, Mary was a sinner. We have reason to believe that Mary was a happy woman. She was happy because she was betrothed. Betrothal was more than engagement. It was a solemn agreement that could be broken only by a bill of divorcement. She was happy because she was in love with Joseph, the village carpenter. She loved him, not because he was rich or handsome, but because she knew he was a good, kind, devoted, gentle man. She was also a woman of unusual faith. When the angel told Mary that she had been chosen of God to be the mother of Jesus, the Son of God, she responded, " 'I am the Lord's servant, and I am willing to do whatever he wants. May everything you said come true' " (Luke 1: 38, TLB).

This left Joseph with a human problem. Mary hurried to the highlands of Judea to visit her cousin Elizabeth. When she returned to her hometown about three months later, Mary was found to be pregnant. Joseph's reaction probably followed normal human patterns—from cold unbelief to open rage, and finally, to stunned amazement. Two alternatives were open to him. He could either expose Mary before the court or divorce her privately. Love caused him to decide on the latter. If ever a man needed a word from God, Joseph did. The word came. One night as Joesph lay considering all that had happened, an angel spoke to him. " 'Joseph, son of David, . . . don't hesitate to take Mary as your wife! For the child within her has been conceived by the Holy Spirit' " (Matt. 1:20, TLB). Joseph was also a person of great faith. When he awoke, "He did as the angel commanded, and brought Mary home to be his wife" (Matt. 1:24, TLB).

In due time Jesus was born. Little can be done to romanticize the Gospel accounts of the human birth. Mary decided to make the eighty-mile trip to Bethlehem. She did not wish to be away from Joseph when her child was born. A bedlam of noise filled their ears as they made their way to the village inn, already crowded to overflowing. Joseph bedded his wife down in the area provided for animals. The delivery room was a stable. No physician stood by.

Only the calloused hands of a carpenter—hands made tender by love—came to her aid. The crib was a manger. With unsurpassed beauty and amazing restraint Luke recorded that Mary "gave birth to her firstborn son; she wrapped Him in cloths and laid Him in a manger" (Luke 2:7, NASB). Jesus' birth was a human birth.

His life was a *human life*. John testified that Christ became a human being—took upon himself human nature—and lived here on earth among us. (See John 1:14.) As a man, Jesus possessed all the essential elements of human nature.

As a man, Jesus was subject to the laws of human development. In infancy and childhood he consciously limited himself, making it necessary for him to grow and mature as all other people. Luke recorded that Jesus grew physically and mentally, and was loved by God and man. (Read Luke 2:52.) It was necessary for Jesus to make progress physically, intellectually, socially, and spiritually because he was subject to the laws of human development.

As a human being, Jesus experienced all the emotions, limitations, and temptations common to us. Can there be any doubt about this when we consider the witness of the New Testament? The Gospel writers recorded times when Jesus was tired, hungry, and thirsty. Jesus experienced weariness and physical exhaustion when he sat at Jacob's well. The tears he shed at Lazarus' grave were an expression of the real grief of a sensitive spirit. Jesus felt human sorrow, needed friends, and desired encouragement as does any other person. He experienced love, compassion, anger, anxiety, and fear.

Jesus had to fight the same temptations other people fought. He fought this battle, not only at the beginning when he met Satan in the desert temptations, but to the end of his life. It was not a sham battle fought for our benefit. Some people feel that Christ could not have sinned in these temptation experiences even if he had wanted to. If this were so, his victory would have been easy— almost automatic—and would have been little comfort to us in our temptation experiences.

Jesus' death was a *human death*. His physical suffering on the cross was real. The mental anguish he experienced because his disciples fled was real. The spiritual anguish caused by the Father's rejection was real. This was not the make-believe play acting of a God in human disguise. Jesus was a man—an extraordinary man—whose humanity was undeniable.

As Christians we must hold to the humanity of Christ, because it is crucial for our salvation. If Christ was not fully human, the whole doctrine of redemption falls. "Do you see why?" asked James Stewart. "Suppose we were led to conclude that He was not quite human, . . . not only are we robbed of our most precious pattern and example, but what is far worse, we have to say that God has not come the whole way after all, that God has not quite stooped down to the depth of our urgent need nor borne all our human burden."[2]

When we insist on the full humanity of Christ, we are simply saying that God, in love for you and me, has indeed come all the way. He meets us where we live. He knows all about us and loves us anyway. "There is one . . . mediator between God and men, the man Christ Jesus" (1 Tim. 2:5).

Was Jesus Fully Divine?

For centuries before Jesus came, devout Jews had looked for and predicted the coming of the Messiah. The word *Messiah* is Hebrew for the Anointed One. Ideas of what the Messiah would be like and how he would go about his work greatly differed. But expectation that the Messiah would come was widespread.

Do you remember? On exam day at Caesarea Philippi Jesus asked, " 'Who do you say that I am?'

"Simon Peter replied, 'You are the Christ, the Son of the living God' " (Matt. 16:15-16, RSV). The long-awaited Messiah had come in the person of Jesus Christ.

The incarnation affirms that the man Jesus of Nazareth was in a unique sense the self-expression of God. Paul expressed the idea in his letter to the Colossian Christians: "For in him [Christ] dwelleth all the fulness of the Godhead bodily" (Col. 2:9). Having already affirmed that Jesus was fully, completely, and truly human, we are now ready to affirm that he was fully, completely, and truly divine.

In reading the Gospel accounts, you cannot escape the impression that Jesus Christ is the divine Son of God. There is a sense in which the divinity of Christ can be understood only within the framework of a Christian experience. When we consent to follow him and live for him, we begin to know who he really is. To attempt to *prove* the divinity of Christ to someone who has no interest in the Christian life is often wasted effort. It is within the life of Christian discipleship that we come to a knowledge and appreciation of who Christ really is.

Jesus' birth was a *divine birth*. What would you look for if, at one point in history, God became man? Would it surprise you to learn of mysterious happenings, supernatural events, and a strange mixture of the human and the divine?

If God decided to translate himself into the language of humanity, it should not surprise us to learn that he would make a special entry into the world of time and space. This special entry we call the virgin birth. "Mary asked the angel, 'But how can I have a baby? I am a virgin.'

"The angel replied, 'The Holy Spirit shall come upon you, and the power of God shall overshadow you; so the baby born to you will be utterly holy—the Son of God' " (Luke 1:34-35, TLB). The virgin birth puts the divine and human together. Jesus had a human mother but a divine father. A special person (God) made a special entry (virgin birth) into the human order.

His life was a *divine life*. Many strange happenings in the life of Christ cannot be explained in human terms. These things present problems only for those who embrace a naturalistic religion. For those whose basic stance does not allow for miracles or the supernatural, much that happened in the life of Christ must be explained away. But for those who believe Christ to be the Son of God and the Bible to be a record of his divine activity, no problem exists with the supernatural.

One signpost pointing in the direction of this divine life is the *claim Christ made concerning himself*. On one occasion, the Sanhedrin, the supreme Jewish council, gathered in the home of Caiaphas, the High Priest, to try Jesus. Finally, Caiaphas confronted Jesus with a direct challenge: " 'I adjure You by the living God, that You tell us whether You are the Christ, the Son of God.'

"Jesus said to him, 'You have said it yourself; nevertheless I tell you, hereafter you shall see the Son of Man sitting at the right hand of power, and coming on the clouds of heaven.'

"Then the high priest tore his robes, saying, 'He has blasphemed! What further need do we have of witnesses? Behold, you have now heard the blasphemy; what do you think?' They answered and said, 'He is deserving of death!' " (Matt. 26:63-66, NASB). If Jesus had not made a direct claim to be the Messiah, why was everyone so upset? Somehow on the lips of Jesus this claim seemed entirely fitting, proper, and believable.

A second signpost pointing in the direction of this divine life is the *sinlessness of Jesus*. His friends and enemies turned the brightest searchlights of criticism upon him without finding one flaw in his moral character. There is no record of Jesus ever confessing personal sin. The writer of Hebrews concluded: "This High Priest of ours understands our weaknesses, since he had the same temptations we do, though he never once gave way to them and sinned" (Heb. 4:15, TLB).

A final signpost pointing in the direction of this divine life is that *Jesus is able to do for men what only God can do*. It is generally accepted that miracles, healing powers, and forgiveness belong to God.

The Gospel writers told of a time when four friends brought a paralyzed man and lowered him down right in front of Jesus. "When Jesus saw how strongly they believed that he would help, Jesus said to the sick man, 'Son, your sins are forgiven!'

"But some of the Jewish religious leaders said to themselves as they sat there, 'What? This is blasphemy! Does he think he is God? For only God can forgive sins' " (Mark 2:5-7, TLB).

They were right, of course. Only God *can* forgive sins. But, let's follow the story to its conclusion: "Jesus could read their minds and said to them at once, 'Why does this bother you? I, the Messiah, have the authority on earth to forgive sins. But talk is cheap—anybody could say that. So I'll prove it to you by healing this man.' Then, turning to the paralyzed man, he commanded, 'Pick up your stretcher and go on home, for you are healed!' " (Mark 2:8-11, TLB). The man did as Jesus commanded him.

We are all painfully aware of our need of divine forgiveness. Sin constantly raises a barrier between us and God. What are we to do? Ignore sin and hope the consequences will go away? Remind ourselves that these are only "guilt feelings" not worthy of our attention? No. We confess them to God and claim the divine forgiveness made possible by the death of Christ. Our deepest assurance of divine forgiveness comes when we have encountered Christ. When we experience forgiveness, Christ is doing for us what only God can do.

His resurrection was a *divine resurrection*. No fact proves the divine nature of Christ as does his resurrection from the dead. We have already affirmed his human death. Now we affirm his divine resurrection. The truth is that "Christ died for our sins according to the scriptures; he rose again the third day according to the scriptures" (1 Cor. 15:3-4).

All four Gospel writers record the resurrection. The remainder of the New Testament is given to proclaim it. "The bodily resurrection of Jesus is one of the best authenticated events in all of history," concluded Herschel H. Hobbs in *The Baptist Faith and Message*.

To the early disciples—and to many Christians living now—the resurrection was God's stamp of approval on the things Jesus did and said. As history's most extraordinary event, it proved Christ's claim to a special relationship with God.

A Brief Wrap-up

We must conclude that Jesus is both divine and human. The incarnation, the teaching that God became flesh, takes both ideas seriously. We must hold to both and give up neither. Why?

Suppose you were asked to cross over a bridge broken only at one end. Would it make any difference which end was broken? No. A bridge broken at either end is inadequate. If Jesus were only a man, we would have a bridge broken on the heavenward end. We could never find God through him. If Christ were only a phantom-God appearing on the earth without actually becoming man, we would have a bridge broken on the earthward end. In that case we would have no Savior.

Two questions were asked in the conversion experience of Paul. When the risen Christ appeared to him on the Damascus road, Paul asked, "Who art thou, Lord?" (Acts 9:5). The content of this chapter is intended to answer that question. After Paul received his answer, he asked a second question, "Lord, what wilt thou have me to do?" (Acts 9:6).

One question logically follows the other. When we fully realize that Jesus is the Christ, the Son of the living God, the only worthy response is to ask, "Lord, what do you want me to do now?"

"All we want in Christ, we shall find in Christ. If we want little, we shall find little. If we want much, we shall find much; but if, in utter helplessness, we cast our all on Christ, He will be to us the whole treasury of God."[3]

—*Henry B. Whipple*

Honestly Now

Read Matthew 16:13-16. Place yourself in this group of disciples. During the question time you answer the question, Who do your friends say that I am? Write your answer.

Spend one minute with your eyes closed. Shut out the world. Be alone with your thoughts. Answer the question, Who would you like Jesus to be to you? Share these thoughts with God in prayer.

CHAPTER 3

About the Holy Spirit

Memory Verses: *John 14:16-17; John 14:26* (cards 6-7)

Some people think that reality is what we taste, feel, smell, see, hear, or bump into. Such a philosophy implies that the Holy Spirit cannot be real because he is invisible. Or, as Bernard Ramm has said, "Spirits are hard to get a peek at."[1] No one has ever captured the Holy Spirit in a test tube. Nobody is going to turn over a rock and discover the Holy Spirit. Does that mean he is unreal?

How many times have you seen electricity? Have you ever seen, felt, tasted, or smelled gravity? Isn't it true that our visible world is composed of invisible particles?

Let's admit that the Holy Spirit can be a reality. We begin our search for truth with a study of the nature of $\underline{\pi\nu\epsilon\upsilon\mu\alpha}$

Spirit

The symbol to guide our search will be the dove.

At the baptism of Jesus the heavens were opened and he "saw the Spirit of God coming down in the form of a dove" (Matt. 3:16, TLB).

A Union of Three in One

Put on your hip boots. You can't spend all your life in the shadows. We must talk about the Trinity—the doctrine of the union of three persons (the Father, Son, and Holy Spirit) in one Godhead.

The first two chapters dealt with the nature of God and the nature of Christ. This chapter on the nature of the Holy Spirit completes our study of the Trinity. The doctrine of the Trinity is a mystery, and never can be completely rationalized. Yet, the New Testament is a Trinitarian document. We, therefore, confess that the Father is God, that the Son is God, and that the Spirit is God.

INTERROBANG **?** It is possible to affirm our belief in the Trinity while we continue our search into the rich implications of our Trinitarian faith.

Baptists have been protected from various extremes by their balanced theology of Father, Son, and Holy Spirit. These three are uncreated, equal, and eternal. The diagram should look like this:

A balanced theology insists on equality. Any time a certain group emphasizes one person of the Trinity almost to the exclusion of the other two, the result is extremism.

Extremism

1. Affirming the unity of God

but denying the Trinity

2. Son gets the emphasis

the Father and   the Holy Spirit are minimized

3. Emphasis on Holy Spirit

Father and Son less important

Christians who have emphasized the Spirit while giving little consideration to Father and Son have interpreted "the baptism of the Holy Spirit" as separate from conversion. Some people also have practiced *glossolalia*, speaking in tongues, as the proof that a person has received the baptism of the Holy Spirit. In many cases this has produced emotional excesses, frustration, self-centeredness, and splits in churches. Christians constantly must guard against a "Spiritology" which minimizes the Father and Son.

Christian theology avoids extremes, keeping the three persons of the Trinity in proper balance. That is, it affirms the equality of Father, Son, and Holy Spirit in the Godhead.

How do we explain the mystery of the Trinity? We don't! I found the following illustration helpful, though. Haven't you noticed that in various places in the Bible different persons of the Godhead are in the spotlight? Let's think of the Bible as a drama being acted out on a stage. In the Old Testament, the Father is in the center of the stage, while the Son and the Spirit watch from the wings on either side. In the Gospels, the Son is in the center of the stage, while the Father and Spirit are on either side. Beginning with Acts, the Spirit

39

is in the center of the stage, while the Father and Son are on either side. Yet Father, Son, and Spirit are present at all times, and are involved in both the plot and the action.

A Peek at a Person

Have you noticed? It is easier to think of the Father and Son as persons. Why? Because we have known other fathers and sons who are persons. Have you ever known a spirit who is a person? Some mental effort will be required to accept the Holy Spirit as a person. Let's try it anyway.

The word *spirit* is grammatically a neuter gender. Usually we do not attribute personality to inanimate objects. The Holy Spirit is a person. To grasp this one spiritual truth can transform your understanding of the Holy Spirit. All your future relationships with the Holy Spirit will be with a person. Understanding this concept will require some Bible study.

The Holy Spirit is the third person of the Trinity. We do not believe in three Gods. We believe in one God who bears three relationships to man.

Read the following Scripture passages to discover the personality of the Holy Spirit.

Three ways he has shown himself to man	Genesis 1:2; Matthew 3:16; 28:19
Referred to as a person	John 14:16-17,26; 16:7-15
Things he does:	
strives	Genesis 6:3
comforts	John 14:16-18,26
testifies	John 15:26
reproves	John 16:8
guides	John 16:13
helps	Acts 1:8
Reactions:	
blasphemed	Matthew 12:31
received	John 20:22

resisted	Acts 7:51
grieved	Ephesians 4:30
insulted	Hebrews 10:29
Godlike qualities:	
Present everywhere	Psalm 139:7
All-knowing	1 Corinthians 2:10
All-powerful	1 Corinthians 12:11
Does God's work	Genesis 1:2;
	John 3:5; 16:8;
	Romans 8:11

Do you need power to live the Christian life in a difficult place? Do you need power to accomplish a task that is too big for you? Then you need the Holy Spirit. A small group of disciples huddled together in the upper room to wait for the promise of the Father. After being empowered by the Holy Spirit, they were told to go out and evangelize the whole world. Their task was too great! That same Spirit will give you power to cope and courage to face *your* impossible tasks.

Do you need the ability to communicate effectively your faith to unbelieving friends? Have you longed for the ability to give a testimony that would touch a loved one's heart? Then you need the Holy Spirit. The miracle of Pentecost was one of communication (Acts 2:4-8). Luke observed that the disciples "began speaking in languages they didn't know, for the Holy Spirit gave them this ability" (v. 4, TLB). People of many nations "were stunned to hear their own languages being spoken by the disciples" (v. 6, TLB).

What was happening? Each believer had the ability to tell what God was doing in his life. And every unbeliever had the ability to hear the gospel in a way that he could understand. We desperately need this miracle of communication today.

The Holy Spirit: Alternative to an Empty Life

As a general rule, empty lives do not remain empty. This is the point of an "eerie little parable" Jesus told. It is a story that makes the blood run cold. Ready?

This evil nation is like a man possessed by a demon. For if the demon leaves, it goes into the deserts for a while, seeking rest but finding none. Then it says, "I will return to the man I came from." So it returns and finds the man's heart clean but empty! Then the demon finds seven other spirits more evil than itself, and all enter the man and live in him. And so he is worse off than before (Matt. 12:43-45, TLB).

Jesus used expelled demons to describe the spiritual condition of the people of his day. Let's describe it for our day. Imagine a person who is sick of the way he has been living. He decides he is going to be different—clean up his life. He drives out the impure spirits and bad habits that have caused his unhappiness. He reforms or turns over a new leaf. Things will be different from now on.

Even impure spirits and bad habits need "a place," however. They come back to see how the young person is doing. They discover that their old house is swept, set in order, decorated, *but empty*. They go out and form an alliance with other impure spirits worse than themselves. They return with new force for a complete takeover. The young person is in a worse condition than before.

What was Jesus trying to tell us about life? Empty lives (like empty houses) do not remain empty. Any thief will tell you that breaking into an empty house is easy. Driving out impure spirits and quitting bad habits are not enough. The empty life *will be filled*, either with good or evil.

As Christians, what are we to believe about demon possession? The Bible *avoids* two extremes: (1) complete unbelief in the existence of evil powers and (2) unhealthy interest in their existence to the point of being obsessed. The biblical writers wrote of the reality of Satan as a personal force who stands against man (Job 1:6 to 2:7; Matt. 4:1-11; Luke 10:18). In the Bible, demons are described as invisible, but real spiritual beings (Eph. 6:11-18). At the same time, there is no obsession or unhealthy interest in demons. On the contrary: "God hath not given us the spirit of fear; but of power, and of love, and of a sound mind" (2 Tim. 1:7). *The Christian alternative to demon possession is Holy Spirit possession.*

Too many people live uninteresting lives. They have no priorities, no loyalties, and no sense of commitment. Boredom has set in. This may be caused by many things, among them a negative kind of religion. Have you noticed the number of people who seem to measure their commitment in terms of what they have "given up" for Christ? In other words, a person is a good or bad Christian in terms of demons expelled, bad habits given up, and the list of *don'ts* compiled. But that is not enough! Remember, the main strategy of Satan is not (and never has been) *possession*. His main attack is *temptation*. We need the same power against both.

Because empty lives do not remain empty, the Christian invites the Holy Spirit to come in as indweller, possessor, master. Nothing puts the devil to flight like a positive Christian faith. The serious Christian who is well-anchored in his faith has a remarkable immunity to evil influence.

Your heart was made for divine indwelling. There is a God-shaped vacuum that only he can fill. Jesus said, "Behold, I stand at the door, and knock: if any man hear my voice, and open the door, I will come in to him, and will sup [fellowship] with him, and he with me" (Rev. 3:20). The choice is between evil-possession or Christ-possession.

And Now a Word from Jesus

Jesus taught his followers about the Holy Spirit in his "Farewell Discourse" on the last night before his crucifixion (John 14:1 to 16:33). At this crucial moment you may be sure that Jesus would say *everything* necessary to his disciples' vital Christian experience. Likewise, he would leave out *nothing* necessary to their understanding of who the Holy Spirit is and what he does.

Five special sayings are recorded in these three chapters of John. Each is marked by the repeated use of the title *Comforter* (*paraclete*) for the Holy Spirit. This term helps us understand how Jesus saw the Holy Spirit. In this sense, Comforter literally means "one called along side of." The idea is that of a lawyer for the defense or one who pleads another's case. Jesus saw the Holy Spirit as a divine strengthener, encourager, enabler. When he comes in, he takes away our inadequacies and enables us to cope.

In the first saying, *the Holy Spirit is presented as "the spirit of truth"* (John 14:15-18). You may wish to leave your Bible open to this passage for the following discussion. Notice that the work of the

Spirit will be consistent with the work of the Father. Jesus prays and the Father gives. The Spirit will be "another Comforter" of the same kind as Jesus; therefore, what Christ had been to his followers, the Spirit will be now. The work of Jesus was limited and restricted as to time and place. Not so with the Holy Spirit. He will abide with the believer for ever (v. 16).

In verse 6 of this chapter, Jesus called himself "the way, the truth, and the life." Later he presented the Comforter as "the spirit of truth." Christ was the truth about God, revealed objectively in a human life. The Holy Spirit is the truth about God, revealed in Christian experience. Of course, it is possible to slam the door of the mind against this truth. The fact remains that visible companionship (Jesus) has become inner communion (the Holy Spirit, v. 17). Jesus promised, "I will not leave you comfortless [*orphanous*]: I will come to you" (v. 18). Many people thought that the crucifixion was the end of Jesus, but he is alive, well, and at work in the lives of people.

We desperately need what the Holy Spirit gives. The greatest problems we face are overcome by the Spirit's presence. The Spirit's promise is: "I will never leave you without a friend. I will come to you." You need never be alone!

In the second saying, Jesus described the Holy Spirit as *our teacher in the school of Christian maturity* (John 14:25-26). Jesus clearly identified the Comforter: "by the Comforter I mean the Holy Spirit" (v. 26, TLB). Jesus also declared that the Father would send the Comforter "in my name," with full authority to declare the message of Jesus. This means that the ministry of the Holy Spirit always will be consistent with the ministry of Christ. In other words, you may be called on to be a "fool for Christ's sake." But don't do foolish things and blame it on the work of the Spirit.

Christ's intention is that the Spirit will do two basic things for us. First, *he shall teach you all things* (v. 26). The Holy Spirit will continue the teaching ministry of Jesus. The word *disciple* means pupil or learner. Becoming a Christian is an enrollment—not graduation. Jesus made a beginning with us. We have much to learn. It is the Holy Spirit, our Master Teacher, who keeps us wading deeper, farther, on and on. To spend all of your Christian life wading only ankle deep in the spiritual shallows is a tragedy.

In the second place, the Holy Spirit will *bring all things to your remembrance* (v. 26). The Spirit continues to bring to remembrance things we have let slip. Most of the time we need reminding more than informing.

One of our problems is ignorance. We cannot blame God. He has given us the Comforter with a dual assignment: (1) to teach us all things, and (2) to help us remember what we have forgotten. Have you asked the Holy Spirit to be your teacher in the school of Christian maturity?

The mission of the Holy Spirit is stated in the third "Comforter" saying (John 15:26-27). *His mission is to magnify Jesus.* Notice the order of procession. The Holy Spirit comes from alongside the Father and the Son (v. 26). His work is to magnify Jesus: "He shall testify of me" (v. 26).

An interesting question emerges at this point. When I claim the presence of the Holy Spirit, will I magnify spiritual gifts I have received? Will I magnify myself or will I magnify Jesus? The supreme test of things attributed to the Spirit is, Do these things magnify Jesus?

When the story of Jesus is told, the Holy Spirit makes us feel that it is truth. This is witness from the divine side. The individual Christian also is commissioned to magnify Jesus: "Ye also shall bear witness" (v. 27). This is witness from the human side.

The Holy Spirit's presence is the answer to life's most pressing problems. Do you lack power when you witness to unbelievers? Do you find yourself trying to accomplish spiritual goals in the power of the flesh? "My problem is lack of power," you say. Have you claimed the power of the Holy Spirit? This is our wonderful privilege.

In the fourth saying, we are introduced to the Holy Spirit as *the cross-examiner of the unbeliever* (John 16:5-11). These verses answer the question, What may we expect the Spirit to be doing in the life of the unbeliever? Jesus began this section with some amazing words. "It is expedient for you [to your advantage] that I go away" (v. 7). Can you imagine? All our lives we have wished for the opportunity to see Jesus. We would like to ring his doorbell and ask him a few questions.

How could it possibly be to our advantage that Jesus go away?

Let's hear him out: "For if I go not away, the Comforter will not come unto you; but if I depart, I will send him unto you" (v. 7). Jesus was going away in a visible, bodily sense (limited by time and space). He would return in the form of the Holy Spirit, no longer limited by time and space. Now he is able to influence *all* people in *all* places at *all* times.

With regard to the unbeliever, the Holy Spirit has a special assignment: "And when he is come, he will reprove [convict, convince] the world of sin, and of righteousness, and of judgment" (v. 8). He will cross-examine the unbeliever until he sees and openly admits his sin.

Have you ever tried to convince someone that he is a sinner? You failed, right? Convincing is the work of the Holy Spirit. We must permit him to do his work. First, he convicts people of their sin, "because they believe not on me [Jesus]" (v. 9). When men first crucified Jesus, they did not believe that they were sinning. Later, the crucifixion was preached and they were "pricked in their heart" (Acts 2:37). How do you explain the difference? The Holy Spirit was doing his work.

He also convinces the unbeliever of righteousness, "because I go to my Father" (v. 10). When men first looked at the cross, it looked as if righteousness had failed. Later, a centurion looked at the same cross and said, "Truly this was the Son of God" (Matt. 27:54). How do you explain the difference? Could it be that the Spirit was at work?

Finally, he convinces people of the certainty of judgment, "Because the prince of this world [Satan] is judged" (v. 11). When men first looked at the cross, they thought Jesus had been judged and condemned. Later they saw that, in reality, it was Satan himself who had been judged and condemned. How do you explain the difference? The Holy Spirit was doing his work.

The Holy Spirit provides what we need most. For the unbeliever he provides the evidence of sin which brings the conviction necessary for conversion. For those of us who are his witnesses, he goes before us to convince or convict the unbeliever of his need for conversion. To convince men that they are sinners is his work—not ours.

In the last saying, the Holy Spirit is presented as *the living pres-*

ence of Christ for today's world (John 16:12-15). Jesus expressed a dilemma which every Christian teacher feels at one time or another, "I have yet many things to say unto you, but ye cannot bear them now" (v. 12). Apparently, the disciples were not mature enough at this point for some truths. God reveals to us only as much as we can understand and put into practice.

If some truth is being deliberately withheld—to be revealed to his disciples at a later time—how will it be revealed and whose responsibility will it be? The answer is found in verses 13-15. The Holy Spirit, the living presence of Christ, will continue and complete the training Christ began. Their work is the same. Their authority is the same: "For he shall not speak of himself [on his own authority]; but whatsoever he shall hear, that shall he speak" (v. 13). Their purpose is the same: "He [the Spirit] shall glorify me [Jesus]" (v. 14). Their teaching is the same: "He shall take of mine, and shall shew it unto you" (v. 15).

The Holy Spirit is not to be thought of as an agent acting independently of and apart from Christ. He is working jointly with and dependent on Christ. The ultimate outcome of their work will be the same. If you are involved in some activity that is not consistent with the life and teachings of Jesus, do not blame it on the Holy Spirit.

In these five sayings, we have sought what Jesus had to say about the Holy Spirit. It is true that neither the "baptism of the Spirit" nor speaking in tongues has been mentioned. Note that Jesus made reference to neither in his "Farewell Discourse" to his disciples. He was speaking on the night before his crucifixion. At that crucial moment, Jesus explained clearly who the Holy Spirit is and what he does.

Tying up Loose Ends

My purpose in this chapter has been to explore the doctrine of the Holy Spirit. My hope is that the Spirit will be more real and, therefore, more believable. When the Spirit comes into focus for you, your spiritual life will take on more meaning.

The Holy Spirit is a person. Our relationship to him is a personal one. The Spirit is the member of the Trinity *who touches us.*

We need what the Holy Spirit can give. Let's do a brief recap on what the Holy Spirit is to the believer. What can we expect him to do for us?

He gives personal power (Acts 1:8).

He gives boldness in witnessing (Acts 4:8-13).

He is our divine Counselor (John 14:1 to 16:33).

He takes up permanent residence within us (John 14:17).

He is our personal teacher (John 14:26).

He is our instructor to complete the training Christ began (John 16:12-15).

That is not bad for a beginning! The possibilities are unlimited. Did you know that *the New Testament frequently associates the Holy Spirit with love?* (See Rom. 15:30; Col. 1:8; 2 Tim. 1:7) Because the Spirit is a person, he is capable of loving as are the Father and the Son. Love is listed as a part of "the fruit of the Spirit" (Gal. 5:22).

Paul said, "God's love has been poured into our hearts through the Holy Spirit" (Rom. 5:5, RSV).

CHAPTER 4

What Is God's Purpose for People?

Memory Verses: *Psalm 8:5-6; Romans 7:22-23* (cards 8-9)

We now turn our attention to a study of the nature of

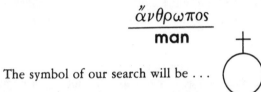

The symbol of our search will be . . .

The previous chapters have affirmed God's desire to be known and his revelation of himself in his Son, Jesus Christ and through the Holy Spirit. But why all this interest in people? Why would God go to so much trouble to be known by human beings?

The psalmist had the same problem in mind when he observed: "When I look at the sky, which you have made, at the moon and the stars, which you have set in their places—what is man, that you think of him; mere man, that you care for him?" (Ps. 8:3-4, GNB). What is God's purpose for people? We are all looking for the answer to that question.

I BELIEVE THAT MAN IS A CREATURE OF WORTH. For me, this is a truth that makes a difference. I don't pretend to understand all the complexities of human nature. Neither do I pretend to understand all the mysteries of God's dealings with people. But, that doesn't disturb me.

INTERROBANG. **?** It is possible to affirm our belief in the worth of the individual while we continue our search for greater understanding of the nature of people.

49

Before proceeding, take a minute to write one brief sentence stating your understanding of God's purpose for people.

_____

_____

_____

Life is an amazing blend, harmony, and integration of body, mind, and spirit. Man is a composite of the physical, the psychological, and the spiritual. To be a human being is a difficult and complex thing. There is some question as to whether the human race is up to it yet.

As a Christian today, you are living in confusing times. The field of knowledge is expanding with breathtaking speed. The future becomes the present so rapidly it leaves us in a state of shock. To make bad matters worse, we hear conflicting reports about mankind.

Homo Sapiens or Homo Mechanicus?

Is a person a human being or a human machine? Is a person determined by his past or free to choose against his past? Does environment and heredity determine a person's choices, or is he responsible for his behavior? The answer to these questions is crucial in understanding human nature.

Individuals are exposed to numerous fields of knowledge which, in varying degrees, support the idea that people function as machines. Within these disciplines a person is considered a creature of law, a victim of heredity, or a product of his environment. Carried to extremes people become objects or robots, without human value and prone to fatalism. This view allows no freedom for God to interact with a person and no room for personal responsibility for chosen behavior.

One of the great dangers of this age of science, technology, specialization, and professionalism is that we may lose our sense of the importance of the person. People may become automatons, statistics, cogs in a massive wheel, a file folder, a number, or a card in a roll book.

Most of us have experienced the empty feeling that follows being dehumanized—treated as though we were less than humans. We resist automatic lives, robot-like movements, and the treadmill of meaningless activity where no one takes the slightest interest in us *as persons*.

The twentieth century has presented us with a new problem— the population explosion. On every hand we are confronted with wall-to-wall people. Yet, the irony is that people are lonely. In the middle of great crowds of people, one person can live isolated in unbelievable spiritual solitude.

INTERROBANG. **?** We affirm while we search. We know, but we don't know. At times we are confused by our own actions. We are not as bad as we could be; nor are we as good as we should be. This journey toward self-discovery will be lifelong. Along the way we will experience both the low moments of discouragement and the high moments of rich personal satisfaction.

Answers to the question, Who am I? are numerous. Recent thinkers have swayed masses of people by their views of person-hood. Darwin understood and explained man under biological categories. Nietzsche insisted that people are governed by impulse and instinct. Marx equated the idea of man with the ideal of society. Freud saw people as essentially sex instincts. As a result, man has marched fearlessly backward to a worship of blood, power, and sex comparable to pre-Christian days. The words *responsibility* and *accountability* are missing from human behavior. The above concepts recognize no Godward dimension.

We must admit that we are wonderfully made and very complex. On one hand, we are obviously influenced by our past. There is a sense in which past experiences influence present behavior. On the other hand, the Christian gospel insists that we are free to choose against or rise above our past. Present behavior is not dictated or determined by past experience. A person is constantly aware of his freedom to choose.

One individual described the paradox: "The thing that amazes me about human beings is the goodness of some pretty bad people and the surprising badness of some otherwise good people."

The field of great literature reveals repeatedly the complexity of human personality. People are continually torn between two worlds. Robert Browning commented, "Men are not angels, neither are they brutes." Ralph Waldo Emerson said, "Man is a god in ruins. . . . Every man is a divinity in disguise, a god playing the fool." The noted American humorist Will Rogers observed, "God made man a little lower than the angels, and he has been getting a little lower ever since." Blaise Pascal spoke of man as "a confused chaos! . . . the glory and the scandal of the universe!"[1]

Are People Essentially Good or Evil?

Belief in the essential badness of people is easy to establish. We are born with an inclination toward sin. Later, when the option of choosing good or evil is before us, we deliberately and willfully choose the way of sin. Paul concluded that "all have sinned and come short of the glory of God" (Rom. 3:23).

When we look within our own lives, we find further proof that all have sinned. We are amazed at the gap between what we are and what we ought to be. Sometimes we are even afraid of ourselves, afraid of the forces at work within, and afraid of the actions of which we feel ourselves capable. The doctrine of depravity does not mean that man is totally bad. It does mean that a person is limited, unfinished, sinful, and if left to himself, not capable of much progress.

The purpose of William Golding's book *Lord of the Flies* is to expose this basic defect in human nature. What will become of a person left entirely to himself without any authority or restraint? What is the result of "doing what comes naturally"? What if every individual "did his own thing"? What might we expect?

Golding told of a small group of English lads, brought up in nobility, who were fleeing atomic warfare. Their plane crashed on a lonely island. The pilot died in the crash.

These young lads faced existence without adult influence. On this island there were no parents, no schools, or policemen. They faced the complete absence of law, authority, and discipline. They had to establish a new order. What would they do?

Ralph began to emerge as leader. He used a shell as a megaphone to call meetings. He served as a constant reminder of what they had been and ought to be. He symbolized past experience and common sense. He became the conscience of the group.

Piggy was a short, fat boy with thick glasses. He was an intellectual and served as a reminder of the place of reason in establishing a new order. He was treated as an outsider and was gradually rejected by the group. In a struggle late in the book, Piggy's thick glasses were broken, symbolizing the final break with intellect. Piggy was ultimately killed by the group.

As the story progressed, Jack emerged as leader of the hunters. At first he innocently hunted and killed pigs for food. He developed a love for killing. He was more emotional and symbolized the necessity for skill. Before the story ended he had painted his face and, behind this mask of liberation, became a bloodthirsty savage.

At first the boys felt an uneasiness in their wrongdoing. Ralph tried in vain to keep a fire going. No one was interested enough in being rescued to help him. Things began "breaking up," "going rotten." Rules were rejected without concern. Savages emerged. They began to live like animals. There was no message from the grown-up world.

On one occasion Ralph said to Piggy, "What's wrong with us? What makes things break up like they do?" Later on, the "Lord of the Flies" (a translation for the Hebrew word for devil) explained to Simon, the mystic, " 'You knew, didn't you? I'm part of you? Close, close, close! I'm the reason why it's no go. Why things are what they are.' "[2]

Finally Jack (the savage) began to hunt Ralph (the conscience of the group) to kill him. About that time a ship landed on the island. Ralph ran and wrapped his arms around the British naval officer's legs. The captain looked at the wild, painted savage hunters and said: " 'I should have thought that a pack of British boys—you're all British, aren't you?—would have been able to put up a better show than that' . . . And Ralph wept for the end of innocence."[3]

On the other hand, there is considerable opinion and much evidence that *people are good*. The average person does not think of himself as a sinner. He thinks of himself as a fairly good person who, now and then, makes a mistake. He thinks of God as an indulgent, heavenly being standing by to forgive.

Looking in certain areas, considerable optimism concerning mankind can be found. Psalm 8 has been rewritten to read: "O man, how excellent is thy name in all the earth! Who hast set thy glory above the heavens. . . . When I consider thine inventions, the work of thy fingers, the aeroplanes and atomic bombs which thou hast made, what is God that I should be mindful of him, or the Son of God, that I should reverence him?"[4]

We must resist all efforts to make man a god in disguise. The author of Psalm 8 had an exalted view of man because he had an exalted view of God. Our understanding of human nature is largely determined by the kind of God we have.

While some people insist that people are made "a little higher than the beasts," the psalmist proclaimed that God has made man "a little lower than the angels" (Ps. 8:5). Or, as the Revised Standard Version translates it a "little less than God." We must resist any idea that people are merely the highest form of animal life giving expression to natural passions and impulses. On the other hand, we must resist any concept that makes man a god deserving praise for his human achievements. The glory belongs to God—not mankind.

What Does the "Image of God" Mean?

In the biblical view, a person is not the most highly evolved of the animals; he is a special creation of God. A person is not merely a physical and mental machine; he is also "spirit and soul and body" (1 Thess. 5:23), because he has been created in the image and likeness of God. (See Gen. 1:26.)

What does it mean that man is created in the "image of God"? Dimension has been added: "Then God said, 'Let us make man in our image, according to our likeness;' . . . and God created man in His own image, in the image of God He created him; male and female He created them" (Gen. 1:26-27, NASB).

People are different, unique, special creations of God. They have more affinity with the Maker than with the made. They are capable of thinking God's thoughts after him. They can rejoice in that in which God rejoices. The greatest wonder, short of God, is the mind of a human being.

The image of God in a person has nothing to do with physical image. We are not God's look-alikes. It was established in chapter 1 that God is spirit. (See John 4:24.) This means, among other things, that God is invisible. He cannot be seen by the human eye. God does not have a physical body with human characteristics.

What distinguishes the God of the Bible from the divinities of other religions is that he is a personal God who speaks personally to people. What distinguishes people from the rest of created beings is that they are capable of fellowship with other persons and of communication with a personal God.

God created you as a person of worth. God is interested in you. He cares what happens to you. He is for you and not against you. His basic stance toward you is a stance of love. As a person, created in the image of a personal God, you possess tremendous potential for which you will be held accountable.

The Dilemma

So far we have established that people are basically good and evil. They have an amazing capacity to be both.

This struggle between good and evil continues after a person becomes a Christian. On one hand is the lower nature constantly pulling downward toward a life of sin and selfishness. On the other hand, the higher nature constantly draws us upward toward a life of selflessness and spiritual victory.

R. Lofton Hudson described the lower nature as the "man in the basement." This secret self, aggressive and untamed, is constantly trying to break out, and demands constant watching. The more the "man upstairs" (conscience) is controlled by the Spirit of God, the more the Christian will be victorious over the "man in the basement" (lower nature). "But the whole problem of salvation and Christianity," concluded Hudson, "is bringing this man in the basement under control and into cooperation with God."[5]

We take a giant step toward spiritual maturity when we accept this tension between the lower and higher nature as a lifetime struggle. Every Christian will experience decisive spiritual victories won by his faith in Christ. He must never assume, however, that past victories immunize him against constantly recurring battles and struggles with the man in the basement.

Paul tried to warn us that the new life in Christ is no snap. Speaking naturally and sincerely out of his experience, Paul described the civil war raging within him: "We know that the law is spiritual; but I am unspiritual, sold as a slave to sin. I do not understand what I do. For what I want to do I do not do, but what I hate I do. And if I do what I do not want to do, I agree that the law is good. As it is, it is no longer I myself who do it, but it is sin living in me" (Rom. 7:14-17, NIV.)[6]

Paul had to admit that there were times when he didn't even understand his own actions. The struggle continued: "I know I am rotten through and through so far as my old sinful nature is concerned. No matter which way I turn I can't make myself do right. I want to but I can't. When I want to do good, I don't; and when I try not to do wrong, I do it anyway" (Rom. 7:18-19, TLB). Does this struggle sound familiar?

Many people argue that Paul was describing his condition before he became a Christian—not after. Just to be honest, I am aware of the conflict Paul described as a present, continuing fact in my Christian experience. Aren't you?

Most of us identify with Paul's description of the dilemma. "It seems to be a fact of life that when I want to do what is right, I inevitably do what is wrong. I love to do God's will so far as my new nature is concerned; but there is something else deep within me, in my lower nature, that is at war with my mind and wins the fight and makes me a slave to the sin that is still within me. In my mind I want to be God's willing servant but instead I find myself still enslaved to sin. So you see how it is: my new life tells me to do right, but the old nature that is still inside me loves to sin" (Rom. 7:21-23, TLB).

Paul felt as though he were a split personality, two men in one skin, a walking civil war. You and I have felt this often. We are never as good as we know we ought to be. Is there any hope then? Or, do we just give up and sin boldly?

The Christian life can be a victorious life. Paul discovered a reason for hope when he said, "What an unhappy man I am! Who will rescue me from this body that is taking me to death? Thanks be to God, who does this through our Lord Jesus Christ! (Rom. 7:24-25, GNB). Our deliverance may be partial and incomplete now because of the continuing influence of the lower nature, but victory is possible! Christ is the resource for victory in the Christian life.

Salvation does not deliver us completely and entirely from the lower nature. Growth toward Christian maturity consists in submission to the Spirit's control and in the strengthening of our conscious controls. The living presence of Christ within strengthens our inner resources against temptation. Christ saves the whole person, but the "man in the basement" is not completely destroyed. The lower nature must be kept under control by the Spirit of God working through the Christian. The more we submit to the control of the Holy Spirit, the more we are able to control our aggressive, untamed impulses. The more we submit to the influence of the lower nature, the more our lives are characterized by sinful and selfish behavior.

The Christian wins victory after victory, but he never quite destroys the foe. Those who continue to struggle against temptation are growing. Those who give up are pathetic. Only in the future is our victory really complete. Only in heaven will we be completely delivered from the presence of sin and the impulses of our lower nature. Present victory is possible only as we submit to the control of the Spirit. And, Christ does expect us to be victorious!

What Happens in Conversion?

It has been said that we would rather die than really be known. Nevertheless, I am convinced that the true nature of a person is really worth knowing. Since a person is created in the image of God, "a little lower than the angels" (Ps. 8:5), he possesses a potential and purpose we must understand and appreciate.

A person has potential for both bad and good. He may be converted to the unworthy as well as to the worthy. When a person persists in going his own way, things do fall apart and go rotten. Selfish living results in lost direction, destiny, or purpose. Knowing much about pleasure, we know little about joy. Knowing much about ease, we know little about peace. What is left is a "God-ache" in the heart. We have discovered by personal experience the necessity of conversion.

A person's greatest potential lies in his freedom of choice. That is what makes him responsible before God. God loves us too much to violate our freedom to choose. He places the alternatives before us and waits: "See, I have set before you this day life. . . . and death, blessing and curse; therefore choose life, and that you and your descendants may live" (Deut. 30:15,19, RSV).

Jesus took up the theme: " 'Heaven can be entered only through

"We are, after all, like lumps of clay. There are brittle pieces, hard pieces. We have little shape or beauty. But we need not despair. If we are clay, let us remember there is a Potter, and His wheel."[7]

—Peter Marshall

the narrow gate! The highway to hell is broad, and its gate is wide enough for all the multitudes who choose its easy way. But the Gateway to Life is small, and the road is narrow, and only a few ever find it' " (Matt. 7:13-14, TLB). The choice is yours.

Each of us is faced with the choice between a life that is only physical or a life that adds the spiritual dimension. Jesus described the alternatives to Nicodemus: " 'I am telling you the truth: no one

58

can see the Kingdom of God unless he is born again. . . . A person is born physically of human parents, but he is born spiritually of the Spirit. Do not be surprised because I tell you that you must be born again' " (John 3:3,6-7, GNB).

This is the good news! Human nature can be changed. Lives are being changed. This is our hope! People are becoming new creations; old things are passing away; all things are becoming new. (See 2 Cor. 5:17.) A person does not have to go on like he is. Miracles continue to take place.

What is meant by conversion? We are talking about that process, gradual or sudden, by which an individual commits the direction of his life unto God's leadership. It is a total surrender to God's will; a total dedication of oneself to God. Conversion is accepting fellowship with Christ as life's highest good. It is a deliberate and willing choice to be a follower of Jesus Christ.

Human personality is such that we have a capacity for conversion. It is mankind's greatest need. When this spiritual dimension is not found, people will fill the vacuum with unworthy substitutes. When conversion takes place, Jesus does not take our humanity away from us; he comes down into it, so that we can bring our temptations and failures to him. This helps us maintain our fellowship with him. The next chapter deals with the process of conversion.

Honestly Now

Describe the war going on within you. _____

_____

_____

What are your areas of greatest conflict? _____

_____

_____

Make a list of qualities and traits that you would like to have in your life. Pray, asking God to help you work on these.

CHAPTER 5

What Happens in Conversion?

Memory Verses: *John 3:5-6* (card 10)

Debbie was a bright-eyed fifteen-year-old. Had I been able to pick her brain, I would have discovered mostly question marks. She came to the point abruptly! "I don't understand this conversion stuff. And why do you have to baptized?" She had not attended church much. Her knowledge of the Bible was skimpy.

The next thirty minutes were spent in laying a foundation for Christian conversion. We discussed such questions as: Why is conversion necessary? What happens in conversion? What does it mean to be a Christian? The purpose of this chapter is to explore with you the questions discussed with Debbie. Let's look at conversion.

We continue our search for truth with a study of

the γεννηθῇ ἄνωθεν

The symbol to guide us will be the cross.

Let's Define Our Terms

Words (like *happiness*) mean different things to different people. Part of our problem in describing the process of becoming a Christian is that we use words which do not communicate. We may have some great ideas, but what is their value if we cannot put those ideas into words which people can understand?

The word *salvation* is probably the one used most to describe conversion. Some people speak freely of "being saved" or "getting saved" and feel sure they are being understood. Are they? Do these words communicate to the unbeliever? In the Old Testament the basic idea behind the word *salvation* was deliverance from the problems and difficulties of life. The idea took on a new significance in the New Testament. The emphasis was primarily on salvation from sin. The angel assured Joseph concerning Mary: "She will bear a son, and you shall call his name Jesus, for he will save his people from their sins" (Matt. 1:21, RSV).

Salvation comes from the verb "to restore to health" or "to make whole." Salvation is an experience which makes us whole spiritually. The sick woman who in faith touched the hem of Jesus' garment was "made whole" (literally, saved). (See Matt. 9:20-21.)

Another word that needs defining is *regeneration*. This word describes salvation from the divine side, or what God does for man. Regeneration is the inner change brought about by the Holy Spirit. It is the new birth described by Jesus (John 3:3-7). The new birth is the "divine head start" which the Spirit can give to every person.

Once again words mean different things to different people. Jesus told Nicodemus, "You must be born again."

" 'Born again! exclaimed Nicodemus. 'What do you mean? How can an old man go back into his mother's womb and be born again?' " (John 3:4, TLB).

See the problem? Jesus was talking about spiritual birth. Nicodemus was hearing physical birth. Even Jesus, the Master Teacher, had problems with communication.

The final word is *conversion*, the one used in the title of this chapter. This word describes salvation from the human side or the outward evidence of the inner change. Conversion is that process, gradual or sudden, by which a person commits the direction of his life to God's leadership. Conversion is a deliberate and willing choice to be a follower of Jesus Christ.

Salvation is all-inclusive, describing the total experience. Regeneration is salvation from the divine side, describing the inner change. Conversion is salvation from the human side, describing the outward evidence.

Is Conversion Really Necessary?

Some people seem to live happy, well-adjusted lives without conversion. Our friend Debbie questioned the need for it. Are we to assume that conversion is for everybody? If so, why? What makes conversion necessary? The answer will require a brief review of biblical history. Hang on tight. What follows is the Bible in a nutshell.

The Bible assumes that God exists. He is a holy and just God. In the process of time, he created the universe and man. Man, as the crowning act of creation, was made "in the image of God" (Gen. 1:26-27). This means, above all else, that man was created a person as God, himself, is a person. What distinguishes human beings from the other created beings is that a person is capable of fellowship with other persons and communication with a personal God.

So far, so good. Then sin entered the picture. The holy God created people capable of fellowship and response. He could have made man a puppet, but puppets can't return love. Because he wanted people capable of love, God took a great risk. He gave people freedom of choice. This means that a person is free to love God—or not love him. *Enter sin.*

God had high expectations of the people he had created. He longed for perfect fellowship and a good relationship with them. God desired for people to be holy as he was holy. But a person exercised his freedom of will and *chose against God*. Humanity fell short of what God intended—and that was sin.

One of the favorite New Testament words for sin is a word which means "to miss the mark." You draw the bow. The arrow speeds through the air, falling to the ground before reaching the intended target. It is not merely a matter of missing the bull's-eye; it is not even reaching the target area. That is sin. Paul wrote, "Yes, all have sinned; all fall short of God's glorious ideal" (Rom. 3:23, TLB).

We all have attempted to be God in the drama of life. We are not cast for the role. We try to be the "most important one" and to control people and situations. The result is that the image of God has been blurred. Our relationship to God, if not completely broken, has been badly damaged. We are out of fellowship. We feel strange around him.

OK, a holy God has sinful mankind on his hands. What will he do with them? God must be true to his own nature. His holiness includes both justice and love. What can he do to bring sinful people back and, at the same time, be true to himself? Let's look at the alternative solutions available to God.

In the first place, God could have *measured out punishment in exact proportion to man's sin*. The measuring stick could have been "an eye for an eye, and a tooth for a tooth." Let every person pay the penalty for his sins. This approach would have put justice in the spotlight while ignoring love. God could not accept this alternative and be true to his nature.

As a second alternative, God could have *taken mankind's sin lightly and forgiven all people*, whether or not they desired forgiveness. In this case he would have adopted a policy of leniency, condoning and "winking at" sin. He could have relaxed the standards and excused his favorites. "Well, sin really isn't all that serious," he could have said. But this approach would have put love in the spotlight while ignoring justice. God could not accept this alternative and be true to himself.

Only one alternative remained. God must be just. Mankind is guilty. There is a penalty: "The wages of sin is death" (Rom. 6:23). The penalty must be paid. But, he is also a God of love. How can he express his love for the sinner while showing his dissatisfaction with his sin? *Well, he could pay the penalty himself!* In so doing, justice would be satisfied because the penalty for sin would be paid. Also, love would be manifested in that God paid the penalty he demanded.

This leaves mankind the freedom of choice. He is free to accept or reject God's plan. God loves us too much to violate our freedom to choose. He places the alternatives before us and waits: "See, I have set before you this day life . . . and death, blessing and curse; therefore choose life, that you and your descendants may live" (Deut. 30:15,19, RSV). This third alternative helps us answer another question.

Why Did Jesus Have to Die?

Our need to be forgiven is obvious. But why did Jesus have to die on the cross so that God could erase my sins? If God is all-powerful, surely he could have taken care of sin another way.

In Old Testament days, God's chosen people had difficulty accepting the idea of a suffering servant (Isa. 53:1-12). In New Testament times, Jesus' own disciples raised their voices in shocked disapproval when he spoke of his approaching death. Then the cross became history. Since that time, the unbelieving world has pointed with scorn at a Savior who had to die. All the while the Gospel writers kept saying that the cross was a working out of God's eternal purpose.

Our salvation was within God's purpose. It was God's intention to bring sinful mankind back into right relationship with himself. On the cross, God got under the burden of our sins. "God was in Christ, reconciling the world unto himself" (2 Cor. 5:19).

The concept is not easy to grasp. Human reasoning balks at the idea. Do you mean that God takes our sins so seriously that he came to be crucified—by us—for our sins against him? Do you mean that God loves us so much that he "gave his only Son that whoever believes in him should not perish but have eternal life"? (John 3:16, RSV). Not bad!

Why did Jesus have to die? Perhaps an illustration will help. Let's suppose there is a judge in our town who has a reputation for being both just and loving. A rare combination, indeed. When people are brought before him, they can always count on his fairness and love. He has made enemies on both sides because at times he has been "too just" or "too loving" to suit their fancy.

One day a dear friend of the judge was brought before him for trial. His crime was described. His guilt was proved. The penalty for his misconduct was common knowledge. What would the judge do? He couldn't be lenient even though the man was a close friend. He couldn't be harsh in exacting penalty because of his love for the man. Everyone wondered how he would respond. His enemies thought they finally had him in an impossible situation.

Finally the judge rose from the bench and declared his friend guilty. He went on to describe the penalty in the form of a fine. Then, he took off his robe and stepped down from behind the desk to pay the fine for his friend.

The cross accomplished the same balance of justice and love. Man was a sinner—guilty as charged. The penalty for sin was common knowledge. But God had a reputation for being both just and loving. What would he do? He declared mankind guilty. He described the penalty for sin. Then, he took off his royal robe and

od Is Spirit
hn 4:24

God is a Spirit: and they that
orship him must worship him in
irit and in truth.

Doctrine—God

Word Became Flesh
John 1:14

And the Word was made flesh, and
dwelt among us, (and we beheld his
glory, the glory as of the only
begotten of the Father,) full of
grace and truth.

5 Doctrine—Jesus

---

od Is Light
John 1:5

This then is the message which
e have heard of him, and declare
ato you, that God is light, and in
m is no darkness at all.

Doctrine—God

The Spirit of Truth
John 14:16-17
And I will pray the Father, and he
shall give you another Comforter,
that he may abide with you for ever;
even the Spirit of truth; whom the
world cannot receive; because it
seeth him not, neither knoweth him:
but ye know him; for he dwelleth
with you, and shall be in you.
6 Doctrine—Holy Spirit

---

od Is Love
John 4:8

He that loveth not knoweth not
od; for God is love.

Doctrine—God

The Spirit, Our Teacher
John 14:26

But the Comforter, which is the
Holy Ghost, whom the Father will
send in my name, he shall teach you
all things, and bring all things to
your remembrance, whatsoever I
have said unto you.

7 Doctrine—Holy Spirit

---

sus, the Messiah
atthew 16:16

And Simon Peter answered and
id, Thou art the Christ, the Son
the living God.

Doctrine—Jesus

People, God's Creations
Psalm 8:5-6

For thou hast made him a little
lower than the angels, and hast
crowned him with glory and honour.
Thou madest him to have dominion
over the works of thy hands; thou
hast put all things under his feet.

8 Doctrine—People

Word Became Flesh John 1:14 5 Jesus	God Is Spirit John 4:24 1 God
The Spirit of Truth John 14:16-17 6 Holy Spirit	God Is Light 1 John 1:5 2 God
The Spirit, Our Teacher John 14:26 7 Holy Spirit	God Is Love 1 John 4:8 3 God
People, God's Creations Psalm 8:5-6 8 People	Jesus, the Messiah Matthew 16:16 4 Jesus

The War Within
Romans 7:22-23

For I delight in the law of God after the inward man: But I see another law in my members, warring against the law of my mind, and bringing me into captivity to the law of sin which is in my members.

Doctrine—People

Born Again
John 3:5-6

Jesus answered, Verily, verily, I say unto thee, Except a man be born of water and of the Spirit, he cannot enter into the kingdom of God. That which is born of the flesh is flesh; and that which is born of the Spirit is spirit.

Doctrine—Conversion

Inspired Writing
1 Timothy 3:16

All scripture is given by inspiration of God, and is profitable for doctrine, for reproof, for correction, for instruction in righteousness.

Doctrine—Bible

Pray Always
1 Thessalonians 5:16-18

Rejoice evermore. Pray without ceasing. In every thing give thanks: for this is the will of God in Christ Jesus concerning you.

12 Doctrine—Prayer

Fellowship
Acts 2:42

And they continued steadfastly in the apostles' doctrine and fellowship, and in breaking of bread, and in prayers.

13 Doctrine—Church

From Death to Life
Romans 6:4

Therefore we are buried with him by baptism into death: that like as Christ was raised up from the dead by the glory of the Father, even so we also should walk in newness of life.

14 Doctrine—Baptism

In Remembrance
1 Corinthians 11:26

For as often as ye eat this bread, and drink this cup, ye do shew the Lord's death till he come.

15 Doctrine—Lord's Supper

His Coming Again
John 14:3

And if I go and prepare a place for you, I will come again, and receive you unto myself; that where I am, there ye may be also.

16 Doctrine—Last Things

Fellowship Acts 2:42 13 Church	The War Within Romans 7:22-23 9 People
From Death to Life Romans 6:4 14 Baptism	Born Again John 3:5-6 10 Conversion
In Remembrance 1 Corinthians 11:26 15 Lord's Supper	Inspired Writing 2 Timothy 3:16 11 Bible
His Coming Again John 14:3 16 Last Things	Pray Always 1 Thessalonians 5:16-18 12 Prayer

stepped down from heaven to earth. On the cross he paid the penalty he himself demanded.

I introduce you to one who knew what the cross was all about. He was a particularly notorious criminal in jail at the time Jesus was crucified. He was charged with murder and insurrection. One day he heard the familiar steps of the guard outside his cell. The key turned in the lock and door swung open. The guard said firmly, "Come with me."

They walked together up a narrow dark corridor. The prisoner became fearful. "Where are you taking me?" he asked.

Calmly the guard replied, "You have been set free."

In disbelief the criminal said: "Come on, man! Don't joke about something so serious. Is my execution set for today?"

The guard responded matter-of-factly: "I am serious. You have been set free. Another has paid your penalty. Another has died in your place. You may go now."

Barabbas stepped out into the fresh air and bright sunlight—a free man.

Problems Related to Conversion

The first problem deals with *what kind of experience you expect to have*. When he was fourteen, Richard had confessed Christ and was baptized. A few months later he confided in a youth worker that he was not sure he had been converted. When the friend probed for a reason for his lack of assurance, Richard said, "What happened to me was not anything like what Judy described when she got saved." He doubted because his experience was not like what others described.

Let's establish one fact as a starter: no two experiences are exactly alike. People are different. Some feel more deeply than others. Some pride themselves in being more rational. You see this at a ball game. Two spectators sit side by side. One sits quietly and calmly throughout the game. The other jumps, yells, cries, and screams. But they both *experience* the game.

A second problem is related to *gradual or sudden conversions* to Christianity. To hear some people talk you think their conversion was an "on-the-spot" decision with no prior thought or exposure. Others describe an experience that is more a gradual awakening, like the small bud which slowly opens into the full-grown flower. Both experiences are possible.

The Bible records many different kinds of conversion experiences—all of them genuine. Let's look at three experiences recorded in the book of Acts. The Ethiopian eunuch was the treasurer of North Africa, a man of great authority under the queen. But he was searching for truth. When Philip read to him from Isaiah, and told him about Jesus, the eunuch responded immediately, "I can believe that, and I accept it." His decision was calm and deliberate. He said, "See, here is water! What is to prevent my being baptized?" (Acts 8:36, RSV).

Saul, on the other hand, seemed far from being a Christian. In fact, he was busy persecuting Christians. On the road to Damacus he met Jesus face to face. He saw a bright light and heard the voice of the risen Christ speaking to him. In that one dramatic moment the entire direction of his life was changed—from persecutor to preacher. (Read Acts 9:1-21.) Not every conversion is that dramatic.

In the Philippian jailer we witness the conversion of an outright pagan who had very little background for Christianity. He heard Paul and Silas praying and singing at midnight. He trembled with fear when he thought they had escaped. Upon learning that they were still within the dungeon (when they could have escaped), he said, "Sirs, what must I do to be saved?"

They replied, "Believe on the Lord Jesus Christ, and thou shalt be saved" (vv. 30-31). He believed and was baptized. (Read Acts 16:22-36.)

Each of these conversions is different. Yet, each is valid. We can't wait around trying to conjure up an experience like someone else has described. Nor can we insist that everyone else have an experience exactly like ours. We must allow God to be original with every person. God wants originals—not carbon copies.

The final problem has to do with *the time and place of the conversion experience*. Many people are able to tell you the exact date, time, and place of their commitment to Christ. Others sometimes are disturbed by the fact that their experience was more gradual. They know they are followers of Christ, but they cannot be specific as to time and place of commitment.

An illustration may help dispel the confusion. Falling in love may be either sudden or gradual. For some couples it is love at first sight. Most people discover the experience is more gradual. They grow into love. The day they always remember is their wedding day—not the day they fell in love. Their anniversary is an annual celebration of the day they stood at the altar and said, "I do." Regarding conversion, the day remembered by most Christians is the one on which they made their public commitment or were baptized.

To illustrate further, let's imagine that two men decide to walk from Oklahoma into Arkansas. One man has made a study of the state line and knows exactly where it is. So, with one deliberate step he leaves Oklahoma and enters Arkansas. He knows exactly when that step was taken. The other man, however, is not familiar with the state line. He just keeps walking in the right direction. After a while, he begins to see evidence that he has left Oklahoma and entered Arkansas. Finally, he sees a familiar landmark and says, "I'm now in Arkansas." He cannot tell you the exact time and place of crossing the state line, but *he is in Arkansas, nonetheless*.

To know the when and where of your conversion is helpful. But the most important proof is "the fruit of the Spirit" borne in the daily life as evidence that Christ lives within.

Where Do We Start?

Every journey must have a beginning.

The traditional starting point is *within the church*. When Melanie came to me, she was a walking bundle of problems. In the course of our talking together I asked her if she were a Christian. Her reply was typical: "Well, I suppose so. I am a member of First Baptist Church." Some people assume they are Christians because they are members of a church.

I love the church and have given my life to service through it. At the same time, I recognize that a person is not automatically a Christian because he is a church member. The church is made up of converted people, but it is not a saving institution. Christians are usually committed to the church, but commitment to the church does not make a person a Christian.

The same is true of baptism. When I asked Gary about his relationship to Christ, he said: "I guess I'm not a Christian. I haven't been baptized yet."

The church is made up of baptized people, but baptism did not bring them into right relationship with God. You may ask, "If one has been baptized and has joined the church, isn't that fairly good proof he is a Christian?" Maybe yes. Maybe no.

Many people believe they are Christians (or not Christians) on the basis of *the way they feel*. Thomas said: "When I first became a Christian I had this happy, 'out-of-this-world'-feeling. Now I feel sad, depressed, and ashamed. I guess I'm no longer a Christian."

I have good news! Your relationship to God is not based on feeling. At the moment you trusted Christ, you became a "child of God." Look at your relationship to your parents. Your kinship to your parents is not determined by the way you feel about them.

Haven't you noticed how fickle and changing feelings are? A Christian experiences a wide variety of feelings. Anyway, I have never found in the Bible a statement describing how we are supposed to feel when we are saved. People are different. Some feel more deeply than others. Some are hurt more easily than others. Both joy and sadness come in a wide variety of colors. If our emotions swing like a pendulum, would God accept them as trustworthy proof of our salvation?

Who Is a Christian?

The followers of Christ have been called by many names: disciples, saints, followers of the way. "And the disciples were called Christians [Christ-ones] first in Antioch" (Acts 11:26). The name *Christian* was a label given them by their enemies. What did it mean then? What does it mean now?

What happens in conversion? I have searched everywhere for adequate words and symbols to describe what happens in conversion. My purpose here is to present the "irreducible minimum." Much more could be said. What is the least that can be said? Every conversion experience will be different. What are those factors which are present in every conversion?

Two basic statements that describe what happens in every true conversion are: "A Christian is one who has 'come to himself'—that is, he realizes he is a lost sinner." A Christian is one who has come to the Savior.[1] Christian conversion can be made much more complicated. But it can't be made more simple. These two elements are absolutely essential. Are you a Christian. Let's see.

First of all, a Christian is *one who has "come to himself."* The best illustration of what this means is in a parable Jesus told—the story of the runaway boy. (See Luke 15:11-24.) When the story begins, we recognize the seeds of rebellion. The boy rebelled against the restrictions of home and the repression of external authority. He grew tired of his father stepping in with the house rules. He wanted to be free.

A dreadful fear began to develop—the fear that he would not taste life to the fullest. The boy decided that he would become his own boss. He took what was his and left home.

In the far country he fulfilled his supreme ambition—to do as he pleased. The excitement soon wore off. Everything went horribly flat. Aimless boredom set in. He began to hear the rattle of invisible chains. His situation went from bad to worse. His quest for freedom ended in abject slavery. And bitter laughter went up from the pig pen.

The boy began to compare his present and former conditions. Thoughts of his father's house made it difficult to be satisfied with the pig pen. He also began to look at himself. He didn't like what he saw. At this point, Jesus said that the boy "came to himself." The door was open for repentance—a complete change of mind.

He decided to go back home. His attitude toward home, father, and freedom had changed greatly. The boy was willing to say to his father, "I have sinned against heaven and in thy sight" (Luke 15:21). He found the father watching and waiting—as we always do.

A person realizes that he has failed, and he comes to a new understanding of his real need. Repentance is the result—a complete change of mind about God, sin, and personal responsibility.

A Christian is *one who has come by faith to accept Jesus Christ as Savior.* Coming to Christ is absolutely necessary to the Christian life. (See Matt. 11:28-30; John 1:11-14; Acts 16:30-34; Rom. 10:8-13; 2 Tim. 1:12.) Salvation comes when we, by faith, come to God in the name of Christ. We come believing that God will do what he has promised.

What does it mean to be a Christian? It means at least three things. It means we have entered *a new life*. Jesus spoke of the "new birth" which initiates this new spiritual life (John 3:3-7).

Being a Christian also means *a new relationship*. We have a new relationship with God. We become the children of God—members of his family. We have a new relationship with other Christians. This new family relationship is called the church. You need the church, not to bring you into right relation to God, but to help you grow to maturity in the Christian faith.

Finally, being a Christian means having *a new life-style*. Accepting new conduct does not make you a Christian, but becoming a Christian should make a difference in the way you live. The Christian experience is a life-time process of putting the teachings of Christ into practice in our daily lives.

Are you a follower of Christ? If not, there must be a beginning. Your falling in love with Christ may have been either gradual or sudden. But the time has come for you to say, "I accept Christ as my personal Savior and Lord."

CHAPTER 6

What's So Special About the Bible?

Memory Verse: *2 Timothy 3:16* (card 11)

Another vital area of our search for truth will be the $\underline{\beta\acute{\iota}\beta\lambda os}$
Bible

Many people are asking, "What's so special about the Bible?" Let's seek an answer to that question.

The symbol of our search will be the scroll.

I BELIEVE THE BIBLE IS GOD'S SPECIAL WORD TO MANKIND. I take the Bible seriously, because it is God's true and inspired Word. This is a truth that has made a tremendous difference in the direction of my life. Admittedly, parts of the Bible are difficult for me to understand, and some of it may always remain a mystery. But, that doesn't disturb me.

INTERROBANG **?** It is possible for us to affirm our belief in the Bible as the Word of God while we continue our search for a greater understanding of the unsearchable and inexhaustible riches therein.

The Bible has been called the least-read, best-selling book in the world and "The Book Almost Nobody Reads." To say the least, we purchase it more than we read it, and we praise it more than we study it.

The Bible is a special Book and should have a vital place in the life of every believer.

Special in Its Revelation of God

The Bible is special because it discloses the way in which God seeks to make himself known.

How would you like to receive a personal message from God to guide you in dealing with your problems and to help you make sense out of life? Most of us would appreciate that. May I tell you where you can find such a message?

The Bible is a message from God addressed especially to you. If you read it faithfully, God will speak to you through it, just as personally as if he had sent you a telegram.

When we take the Bible seriously, God himself speaks to us from its pages. The Bible has been called God's love letter to mankind. It contains answers to the basic needs of every heart. The Bible is God's chosen instrument through which his word is spoken directly to us.

Kierkegaard remarked, "We don't read the Bible; it reads us." It reads us like an open book. The Bible is a special book because it helps us to know who and how we are.

The central theme of the Bible is God's disclosure of himself. Sometimes this revelation came through his encounter with a single individual. At other times it involved the nation of Israel as a whole. As you read the Bible, remember that these were real people in a real world who had undergone real experiences with a real God.

Special in Its Makeup

Would you like to understand the Bible better? That should be the ambition of every believer. If you seriously want to hear the voice of God speaking to you through the Bible, you must be willing to read it and to study it carefully and systematically.

Understanding the makeup of the Bible as a whole is a good place to begin. The Bible is a collection of many books. Though it comes to you as one Book with one binding, it is, in reality, a library of sixty-six different books. It has been written by many different authors under different circumstances over a period of a thousand years or more.

Three different languages were employed in writing the Bible: Hebrew, Greek, and Aramaic. The authors were men of varied backgrounds who addressed their books to diverse situations. This means that each book must be understood as a unit.

In a real sense, however, the Bible is one Book. Like the human body, the variety of its parts compose one beautiful unity. This unbelievable unity in the Bible can be explained in one way: the God who reveals himself has one primary purpose—the redemption of mankind.

The Bible has two main divisions, called the Old and New Testaments. The word *testament* means covenant or will. The Old Testament is primarily the book of the Jewish religion and contains God's covenant with his people before Christ. The New Testament is primarily the book of the Christian religion and contains God's new covenant with his people made possible through Christ.

Consequently, our approach to each of these major divisions will be different. The final authority on Christian living is found in the New Testament.

The Bible contains many different kinds of literature. You will understand it better if you know the type of literature you are reading. Are you reading prose or poetry? Are you reading history or drama? Are you reading law or prophecy? Are you reading a letter or apocalyptic literature (like Revelation)?

Perhaps you are reading a passage characterized by the Hebrew fondness for picturesque, figurative, and symbolic language. Any high school English teacher will tell you that the rules for interpretation change with the nature of the literature.

Studying the Bible can be an exciting adventure. To illustrate, use your imagination. Imagine that the Bible is a beautiful building comprised of sixty-six rooms. You have been invited to take a tour. The Holy Spirit will be your guide as you tour the King's Palace. This tour will be hurried. Later you can come back and spend as much time as you like in each room.

First, you enter the spacious vestibule of Genesis where you are introduced to the God of creation. Just ahead are the law courts and a side wing containing the picture gallery of the historical books— scenes of battle, portraits of valiant men, and trophies of travel.

Then enter the schoolrooms. One room is marked "Philosophy" with Job as teacher. Another room marked "Musical Conservatory" is used for a study of the Psalms—some of the best music in all the world.

The upstairs contains a business office where the book of Prov-

What makes the difference is not how many times you have been through the Bible, but how many times and how thoroughly the Bible has been through you. [1]

—Gypsy Smith

erbs governs procedure. Around the corner is the research department headed by brilliant Solomon. The text is Ecclesiastes.

Up on the deck is the observatory where the major and minor prophets peer through a powerful telescope, not so much up into space as down through time, looking for the appearance of the new Star.

Downstairs and across the courtyard, you come into the throne room of the King himself. Matthew, Mark, Luke, and John introduce you to him who is King, Servant, Man, and yet God. You will want to come back often to that room. There is so much to see!

Next, enter the workshop of the Holy Spirit—the book of Acts. In this workshop he is busy making new individuals and a new church and laying plans for world conquest.

Through an open door, see the correspondence office. In there numerous men under the personal direction of the Spirit of Truth are busy writing letters to young churches.

Just before the tour ends, the guide pulls some drapes aside permitting a glance into the unveiling room with a window toward the future. Here you see revelations of glory, adoration, and praise, and catch a glimpse of a new heaven and a new earth.

My hope is that you will come back often for lengthy visits with a prayer for understanding and guidance.

Special in Its Nature

If God is to speak to us through the pages of the Bible, we must have a better understanding of the nature of the Bible. Someone has said that the Bible is a revelation *of* God, *from* God, *to* man, *through* man. This statement reflects the mysterious blend of the divine and human elements in revelation. God speaks to us in the Bible through human authors and human words.

Why God has chosen to communicate through the pages of this particular Book is a question that Christians cannot answer. That God does speak through the Bible is a matter of universal testimony.

God used about forty men as authors in the writing of the books of the Bible. God chose to present his message through human personality. This fact of human instrumentality was recorded by the writer of Hebrews: "Long ago God spoke in many different ways to our fathers through the prophets, . . . telling them little by little about his plans" (Heb. 1:1, TLB). Peter also stated that men spoke from God: "For no prophecy was ever made by an act of human will, but men moved by the Holy Spirit spoke from God" (2 Pet. 1:21, NASB).

When the Bible was written, God worked in the same way he has always worked: namely, through human beings like us. No wonder the Bible throbs with the heartbeat of man. No wonder it is called the drama of human life.

The authors of the Bible were carefully selected and possessed certain qualifications. Yet, they were not robots or stenographers. Each man had his own writing style and was free to inject his own personality into the writing.

For example, the purpose of the four Gospel accounts is to cover basically the same materials—the life of Christ. Yet, each Gospel is distinctly different and reflects the literary style of its author. Consider also the writings of John and Paul. Both were theologians. Yet, their writing styles were widely different. Each wrote in his own way under the controlling power of the Holy Spirit.

The Bible is special because it is divinely inspired. To be a Baptist is to be committed to the Bible as the primary authority in matters of faith and practice. The reason for this is simple. The Bible itself contains numerous claims which suggest its unique inspiration.

The prophets constantly used the phrase "Thus saith the Lord." Another Old Testament passage indicated God's direct involvement in revelation: "The Lord said to Moses, 'Come up to me on the mountain, and wait there; and I will give you the tables of stone, with the law and the commandment, which I have written for their instruction' " (Ex. 24:12, RSV).

Even though no formal definition of inspiration is given in the Bible, the fact of divine inspiration is found often. In the New Testament we read that Paul wrote to Timothy, "The whole Bible (literally, every Scripture) was given to us by inspiration from God and is useful to teach us what is true and to make us realize what is wrong in our lives" (2 Tim. 3:16, TLB).

The word *inspiration* means inbreathed. "To inspire" means to breathe into. In expiration, life goes out. In inspiration, life comes in. By inspiration, then, we mean that the Holy Spirit worked through the human spirit of the writers guiding the process.

The writers were "inbreathed" or inspired by God to write. Peter explained that the Holy Spirit within godly men gave them true messages from God. (Read 2 Pet. 1:21.)

It should not surprise us that the Bible emerges as a Book with both divine and human elements: divine in that it is inspired by God; human in that God chose to present his message through human personality.

The Bible has both divine and human elements. Inspiration, the teaching that God inbreathed or inspired the writers, takes both seriously. We must hold to both and give up neither. Why? Because if we erase the divine element, we argue against the witness of the centuries that the Bible is the Word of God. If we erase the human element, we disregard the divine use of human personality for the communication of that word.

Special in Its Preservation

Carol asked, "How can we say that these sixty-six books are the only inspired books of the Bible?"

Who put it all together? When? On what basis were some books omitted? Have you ever wondered about some of these problems? The time will come when you will wish to make a detailed study of these questions. Resources are available. For now, let me make a few brief observations which might be helpful.

The most remarkable event in the history of literature is the fact that the sixty-six books of the Bible, written by forty or more men over a period of 1500 years, were preserved and ultimately brought together to constitute one great Book. Our theory of inspiration must be broad enough to include preservation. The hand of God was at work preserving these precious writings.

The sixty-six books selected for the Bible form what is called the canon of the Scriptures. The word "canon" means to measure. These selected writings had to measure up to certain qualifications or meet certain tests.

The choice was based on long, careful, and prayerful investigations. We can be sure that each book included in our Bible has passed certain tests and has proved itself to be a part of the inspired

Word of God. Other books written during this time fell short of these tests and were rejected. The process of selection was completed by A.D. 400.

Sometimes, it comes as a shock when people learn that we do not now possess the original manuscripts of any of the books in our Bible. The manuscripts have long since perished.

We do have certain very old manuscripts of the books of both Testaments. They are old enough to be very accurate copies and are of tremendous value. These manuscripts are preserved in libraries over the world and are guarded with greatest care. Recent finds, such as the Dead Sea Scrolls, have provided abundant evidence that the writings we now have are substantially the same as in the days of the first Christian century.

Once again, our theory of inspiration must include preservation. As God was involved in the process of the writing of these books, so was he involved in the process of their preservation until they were brought together in our Bible as we have it today.

Special in Its Purpose

How can God speak his message to us unless we understand the purpose of the Bible? The Christian who wishes to become a good Bible student must recognize the primary purpose of the Bible.

Primarily, the Bible is a Book of religion. The substance of its message is religious. The central concern of the Bible is with man's relationship to God, God's relationship to man, and man's relationship to his fellowman.

Sometimes incidental mention is made of scientific, medical, and psychological matters. In many cases these references show unusual spiritual insight on the part of the writers. On other occasions they reflect the thought patterns of the day in which the book was written. It would be a mistake to turn aside to these matters for purposes of argumentation. The spiritual matters having to do with God's saving activity must be our central concern.

One purpose of the Bible is *that men might believe*. John made this purpose clear when he wrote, "These are written, that ye might believe that Jesus is the Christ, the Son of God; and believing ye might have life through his name" (John 20:31).

The unbeliever should search the Scriptures because they testify of Jesus. They tell how we come into right relationship with God. In the Bible God makes himself known to the unbeliever as a loving and forgiving God. The unbeliever begins to experience life when a sorrow for sin develops and he turns in faith to Christ. Faith is developed and encouraged by listening to and reading the Word of God. (See Rom. 10:17.)

A second purpose of the Bible is *that believers might grow*. So you are a Christian. Now what? Peter urged, "Be like newborn babies, always thirsty for the pure spiritual milk, so that by drinking it you may grow up and be saved" (1 Pet. 2:2-3, GNB).

A baby is not born walking, talking, and eating meat. We must teach him to walk one step at a time and to talk one word at a time. We start him on milk and soft foods; the steak comes later.

When a person becomes a Christian, he is a newborn babe in Christ. He doesn't mature overnight. It will take time to teach him how to walk and talk as a Christian. The new convert should crave the genuine milk of the Word of God because it will help him to grow to maturity in the Christian faith. The steak will come later.

The church does not expect a new convert to be a full-grown Christian overnight. Experience has taught us that it will take time for the maturing process. When you fail, your Christian friends will be standing by, not to criticize, but to give encouragement.

The Bible is one of our main resources for Christian growth. In a farewell message to the Ephesian elders, Paul said, " 'And now I entrust you to God and his care and to his wonderful words which are able to build your faith and give you all the inheritance of those who are set apart for himself' " (Acts 20:32, TLB). By applying the Scriptures to our daily lives, we learn to do God's will. Spiritual growth is the result.

Someone has pointed out that, physically speaking, there are three stages in the maturing process. In the first stage we are fed by others. Our growth is entirely dependent on what others do for us. We move into the second stage when we learn to feed ourselves. We are no longer dependent on others. The final stage comes when we assume responsibility for feeding others. We now have children who are in the first stage and we must feed them.

You are already beginning to see how perfectly this applies to the spiritual life. In our spiritual development we must all go through stage one. For a time our spiritual growth will largely depend on what others do for us (our pastor, Sunday School teacher, or a Christian friend).

It is a great day for everyone when we enter stage two where we begin to assume responsibility for feeding ourselves. At this time we begin to read the Bible because we want to, not because of outside pressures. We begin to pray because we enjoy fellowship with God, not because someone is standing by urging, "Say your prayers." We begin to go to church, not because parents insist, but because we desire to worship God and to fellowship with his people. And, when we are not growing as we ought, we begin to put the blame where it really belongs (on us), and not on "the youth program of the church."

We have reached the final stage in the maturing process only when we begin feeding others. We now have spiritual children who have come to know Christ through us. They are in stage one and are entirely dependent on us for their growth.

The maturing process takes time. God becomes concerned only when we get "locked in" at one stage, when we are not growing. The writer of Hebrews described this common problem: "You have been Christians a long time now, and you ought to be teaching others, but instead you have dropped back to the place where you need someone to teach you all over again the very first principles in God's Word. You are like babies who can drink only milk, not old enough for solid food. And when a person is still living on milk it shows he isn't very far along in the Christian life, and doesn't know much about the differences between right and wrong. He is still a baby-Christian! You will never be able to eat solid spiritual food and understand the deeper things of God's Word until you become better Christians and learn right from wrong by practicing doing right. Let us stop going over the same old ground again and again, always teaching those first lessons about Christ. Let us go on instead to other things and become mature in our understanding, as strong Christians ought to be" (Heb. 5:12 to 6:1, TLB).

How Should This Special Book Be Studied?

Most of us would agree that we ought to study the Bible. In fact, it is absolutely impossible to be the right kind of Christian unless we take time regularly to expose ourselves to the Word of God. Yesterday's food will not sustain us indefinitely; malnutrition is a spiritual as well as a physical problem.

I wish I could offer you a simple formula for Bible reading which would guarantee spiritual growth, but that is not possible. Some people read the Bible without much observable difference in their lives.

Is it possible to be a Bible reader and still not be a good Bible student? The answer must be *yes*. Many Christians have developed habits of Bible reading which, if used exclusively, will not result in a mature understanding of the Bible. It is not that these habits are bad or harmful. It is just that they are inadequate if they represent the only motive for Bible reading.

Let me mention some of these inadequate approaches, giving them humorous titles to aid the memory. They have been collected over many years from numerous sources.

First is the *Santa Claus* approach. The person who uses this approach will spend hours of Bible reading, searching for the surprise element. He will exhaust time and energy on unimportant details which do not result in spiritual maturity. He will try to impress you with all the unusual and sensational "goodies" he has in his bag. This person may be a baby Christian, but you will never catch him up short. He knows the facts!

Next is the *Jigsaw Puzzle* approach. This person is the casual "Scripture-nibbler" who jumps around from one part of the Bible to another, without plan or purpose. While reading he will take a piece from here and a piece from there and try to put them together to mean something. By using this method he can make the Bible say anything he wants.

Then, there is the *Magic Book* approach. In this approach the only time a person goes to the Bible is when he is facing a baffling problem or a difficult decision. He lets the Bible fall open at random and a verse "leaps out" at him and serves as an answer to his immediate problem or decision. Many people give unusual testimonies to the effectiveness of this approach. My point is that an individual will never become a serious Bible student by using this method exclusively.

Others use the *First Aid Manual* approach. In this case the Bible is used for emergencies only. It is placed on the shelf alongside Dr. Spock's books. When certain spiritual ailments are confronted, the Bible is pulled down and the concordance is used to find verses which prescribe a cure.

Finally, there is the old *Rabbit in the Hat Trick* approach. By this method a person puts the rabbit into the hat when no one is looking, and later brings it out, to the surprise and delight of the onlookers. Some people have called this the reverse action approach to Bible study. The process is simple. An individual first determines what he wants to believe. Then, he goes to the Bible to find proof texts for his position.

Someone has suggested that there are basically two types of Bible readers: (1) those who read *into* the Bible what they want it to say, (2) those who read *out of* the Bible what it actually has to say.

If you wish to become a serious Bible student, there is a price you must be willing to pay. Casual "Scripture-nibbling" will not do it. You must be prepared to *read* the Bible and to *study* it with plan and purpose.

The goal of the serious Bible student will be to discover the mind and purpose of the original writer. It is only in discovering what the Bible *meant* that we also discover what it *means*. You can understand the Bible. You only need to be a sincere seeker after truth.

Nothing is quite as suspense-filled and breathtaking to me as the firsthand experience of mountain climbers. How would it be if we approached the task of Bible study with such determination? Both mountain climbing and Bible study require *teamwork*. In Bible study there is great value, at the start, in climbing with a group of experienced climbers.

For a while, success may depend on skillful and experienced teachers who are willing to help others understand the Bible. The Bible study programs in our churches are committed to group study with experienced climbers.

Next, both mountain climbing and Bible study require *special equipment*. The person who is serious about Bible study will need some basic tools. The first step up toward serious study may be as simple as buying a translation which you can understand. Word usage and meaning have greatly changed since the King James Version was translated in 1611. Bible study has taken on a new dimension of inspiration for many people simply by the purchase of modern-language versions.

The next piece of equipment you will need is a one-volume commentary on the entire Bible. A commentary will give you the historical background needed for understanding each book. You will discover such things as authorship, date, purpose of writing, to whom the book was written, and the nature of literature you are reading. The meaning of many passages of Scripture will remain hidden until you have this information.

You also will need a Bible dictionary. This will enable you to look up words and study the grammar, especially in passages that are difficult to understand. By looking up certain names and places you will gain insight into the world of the Bible.

A good study Bible contains a concordance. Learn to use it. It will aid you in finding Scripture passages.

These various tools will aid you in understanding the environment and attitude of the writer. Only after you have discovered the original context are you ready to determine the original meaning.

In both mountain climbing and in Bible study, there are *overwhelming obstacles* to overcome. The first thing you will notice is that some parts of the Bible are easier to understand than others. For that reason you may want to begin with books such as Luke, John, and Acts. Then, read the rest of the New Testament, leaving Revelation until last. Just as the tenderfoot mountain climber does not begin with Everest, the Bible student does not begin with Revelation.

Later, as your skills develop, be prepared to "camp out" indefinitely in those places in the Bible where the going gets rough. Be prepared for times of spiritual drought and extreme exhaustion.

Finally, in both mountain climbing and Bible study, *the goal is always the top*. In Bible study, the top is never clearly defined. In fact, new peaks are always before us. We are facing the "unsearchable riches." Nevertheless, we experience the joy of progress in our understanding of the Bible. Whatever discipline is involved, the reward makes it worthwhile.

There is one basic difference in Bible study and mountain climbing. We will never experience the sadness of the mountain climber—sadness because a great adventure has ended. The task of the serious Bible student is a never-ending one.

Honestly Now

Have you studied your Bible as much as you should? Write out a Bible reading goal. Then list plans to help you reach this goal. Pray that God will help you work your plan.

To Pray or not to Pray

Memory Verses: *1 Thessalonians 5:16-18* (card 12)

Every Christian needs certain disciplines in his life. Just as the physical body must have regular exercise, nourishment, and discipline, so must the spiritual life. We must develop strong, good habits which will expel the weak, evil habits in our lives. For that reason the Christian must always take seriously certain spiritual disciplines—Bible reading, study, prayer, church attendance, and fellowship with other believers.

What Is Prayer?
Some people think that if they pray, everything will be all right. Two approaches to prayer are: (1) to pray and work hard or (2) to pray and do nothing.

Is your life meaningless at times? Do you become bored? Do you ever lose heart? Jesus suggested that Christians "ought always to pray, and not to faint" (Luke 18:1). When you are tempted to give up, you have the option to pray for God's guidance and strength.

What is prayer? Most of us begin with the idea that prayer is talking with God. Sounds simple enough.

After a time of talking with God, prayer may take on a new dimension. We can begin to realize that prayer is a two-way communication. It is more conversation with God than it is a monologue. Prayer is *listening* as well as *talking*. In prayer we actually are seeking to bridge the gap between the human and divine.

As you mature in your Christian life, prayer can become a personal, daily fellowship with a God who loves and cares. It is constant conversation and personal communion. Some people are troubled by the idea that God speaks to us in prayer.

Late one evening during a retreat David rattled the door of my crude cottage and asked, "When you pray, how can you be sure it is God answering and not just your own wishful thinking?" I had no easy answer for David's question.

Basically we rely on the promises of the Bible concerning prayer. God has chosen to communicate with most of us through that "still, small voice" which speaks directly—but without words—to our conscience. The result is a quiet, calm assurance that "This is the way. Walk in it."

Prayer is not pious, empty words piled up so that we can say we have had our quiet time. Simply saying "prayer words" is not enough. Sincerity is more valuable than fancy words. I find some people responding favorably to what is called "conversational prayer." This is an effort to be completely honest and open with God. The result is short, sentence prayers in everyday language. The "Thee's," "Thou's," and church words are omitted. Try this type of praying. You will like it.

Prayer is "the breath of the soul." I like the analogy. Prayer is as necessary to the spiritual life as breathing is to the physical life. But, carry it one step further. We don't get up in the morning, take one deep breath and make it last all day! Breathing is a constant, consistent process. Nor are we to get up in the morning, say a hasty five-minute prayer and make it last us all day! Prayer should become a way of life for us—as natural as breathing. Prayer is the attitude of mind and the atmosphere in which we live. How else do we understand Paul's advice that we "pray without ceasing" (1 Thess. 5:17)?

Does Prayer Make a Difference?

"I tried prayer for a while," Mary said. "But I must not be talking to God in the right way or something. It doesn't seem to do any good."

Some people insist that *prayer cannot do anything*. Prayer cannot possibly make a difference because the universe is governed by inflexible and unchanging laws. This is God's world and his will is bound to be done anyway. What possible difference could it make whether I pray or not?

For such people, the world is like a traffic light. It operates by certain laws. Its changes are planned and timed. The personal desires of the automobile driver or pedestrian have no influence on the light. The light does not turn from red to green simply because we want it to or ask it to.

Other people urge us to believe that *prayer can do everything*. Absolutely nothing is beyond the power of prayer. It makes no difference how bad the problem, how complicated the situation, how impossible the task, all a person needs to do is pray. The remedy is always the same: pray about it.

Such people recognize that the universe is not so inflexible, and behind it all is the Creator who has power over the laws he established. Yet, the Christian must guard against the concept that prayer is a magic show by which we manipulate God into doing things for us. Prayer is not a magic formula by which man can make God jump through hoops. God is not a divine vending machine responding automatically to our desires.

The mature Christian approach lies between these two views. This approach affirms that *prayer does make a difference*! It recognizes that there is something in the universe that responds to earnest prayers. This view takes seriously the biblical promises concerning prayer. At the same time, it rejects the idea that prayer is magical or that God can be manipulated.

We know for certain that prayer brings closer together the one who prays and God. Human conversation makes it possible for us to get to know one another better. We get better acquainted with God by talking with him.

We also know that prayer can bring to pass things which otherwise might not have come to pass. God is not a prisoner in the world he has created. Thinking that God's will is fixed and inflexible is a serious mistake. God responds to our prayers as a Person—not as a machine.

Prayer is not an attempt to force God to do our will; instead it is an effort to be open to his will for us. Prayer is not laying out our stubborn will before God and begging for his stamp of approval; but it is yielding our "want to" for him to mold, alter, or reject to become the same as his will. Prayer is not telling God what to do; it is telling him what we think we need. Prayer is not our effort to change the will of God; rather it is our effort to promote it.

Why Pray at All?

Ed seemed a little uncertain about expressing his true feelings. Finally he came out with what was really bothering him: "If God already knows what we want and need, why tell him? Won't he just give it to us without our having to run to him about every little thing?" There is hardly any Christian alive who has not struggled with that question. The problem is genuine and certainly not easily solved. "Why pray at all?"

My answer to this question will be more a personal testimony than a systematic study. I am happy to report that, after many years of theological education and more than twenty years in the ministry, I still pray. In fact, I find prayer more necessary as the years pass. I would be first, however, to admit that I do not fully understand what happens in prayer.

INTERROBANG **?** It is possible to affirm some things while we continue our search for truth in others. My affirmations are simple: (1) I do pray, and (2) I believe prayer makes a difference. At the same time I admit that I do not understand all that is involved in prayer. I do not pray because I can rationalize it. Neither do I pray because I have all the questions answered and all the problems solved.

"Then why do you pray?" you may ask.

I gladly answer. I make prayer a vital part of my personal Christian life for three basic reasons.

First of all, I pray *because God is real to me*. God is a Person. He made me a person—and not a puppet. A person's highest capacity is communion with his Creator. I pray because God is a real person and my relationship with him is a personal one.

Why go to God with every little thing? Because our relationship is a personal one. Even the human parent wants the child to open up his heart without fear, though most of what is told is already known. Does this mean that family conversation is useless? Of course not! The thoughtful husband expresses his love for his wife from time to time, in spite of the fact that she already knows it. Why? Because it is merely part of what it means to live on a truly personal level. Our prayers are not needed to inform God about things he does not know. They are needed as a recognition of our personal fellowship with the Father.

Second, I pray *because Jesus prayed and taught his followers to pray*. Have you ever thought much about the fact that Jesus prayed? Every time I struggle with the problems related to prayer, I pause and reflect on the fact that Christ actually prayed. He is my Lord and he prayed. He prayed, not to set an example, but because he needed to pray. If prayer was necessary for him, what about you and me?

At their request, Jesus gave his disciples some specific advice concerning prayer. Commonly called the "Lord's Prayer," it should be called the "Disciples' Prayer." Jesus said: "Pray along these lines:

'Our Father in heaven,
We honor your holy name.
We ask that your kingdom will come now.
May your will be done here on earth,
Just as it is in heaven.
Give us our food again, today, as usual,
And forgive us our sins,
Just as we have forgiven those who have sinned
  against us.
Don't bring us into temptation,
But deliver us from the Evil One. Amen.' "
                    (Matt. 6:9-13, TLB)

Most of us have memorized this model prayer. Yet, Jesus never intended that it be repeated over and over until it becomes empty words. He intended that it be a guide by which you measure your own prayer life. Look at it with that idea in mind.

When you pray, do you have any trouble thinking of God as a loving, heavenly Father? Is he understanding, forgiving, approachable? For Jesus, prayer was a conversation between Father and child. "We honor your holy name," reveals proper reverence (v. 9).

Also, Jesus saw prayer as the way God reveals his will to us. It makes a great difference whether you pray "My will be done" or "Thy will be done" (v. 10). It is the difference between a heavenly Santa Claus and a heavenly Father. Prayer is letting God get to you and teach you his will. The ultimate aim is for every person to be personally committed to God's will.

God wants us to tell him what our needs are (v. 11). The "daily bread" request is for more than literal bread. It is a request for all the needs that sustain life. You need more than bread, right? Tell God what you think you need.

Prayer is also a request for forgiveness and the practice of forgiving (v. 12). Each of us needs forgiveness. Why? Because "all have sinned; all fall short of God's glorious ideal" (Rom. 3:23, TLB). One of the New Testament words for sin means "to miss the mark." Many people accumulate much guilt over sins in their lives. What should they do about it? Get rid of it! In prayer ask for God's forgiveness and cleansing. Then say, "Thank you, Lord, for doing what you promised."

But watch that cliff-hanger, "just as we have forgiven those who have sinned against us." When you pray, do you have bad feelings toward others? Do you nurse hatreds and hold grudges? God is under no obligation to forgive us as long as we have not forgiven others. Notice the verses immediately following the "Disciples' Prayer": "Your heavenly Father will forgive you if you forgive those who sin against you; but if you refuse to forgive them, he will not forgive you" (Matt. 6:14-15, TLB).

Finally, according to Jesus, prayer is asking God to protect us from temptations and to deliver us during times of testing (v. 13). Prayer is good preventive medicine. Sometimes it is better not even to be exposed to temptation than it is to try to resist. That is where God and prayer come in. Most of us are like the young man who confessed, "I can resist anything but temptation." In our prayers we should ask God to direct our ways away from temptation.

Jesus saw prayer as being absolutely essential for the Christian. He prayed and taught his followers to pray. For that reason, and others, I have made prayer a habit of my life.

Third, I pray *because of the prayer promises* recorded in the Bible. Christ gave us bold affirmations about prayer. Imagine being a new Christian. You are just beginning to read your Bible for the first time. In the process you stumble onto the following prayer promises: Mark 11:24; Matthew 18:19; John 14:14; Matthew 21:22.

90

I am challenged by the boldness of these promises. Frankly, there are times when they seem not to agree with the facts of experience. When that happens, I do not stop praying. I probe more deeply into Christ's meaning behind these promises.

Where Do I Begin?

One evening I was speaking about prayer to a group of people. I noticed that Thomas was fidgety. His wrinkled brow told me he could hardly wait for the discussion period. I was right. He was the first to speak.

"Pastor," he began, "you assume too much. You must think we already know how to pray. I don't know about the others, but I don't know how to pray. I don't even know where to begin."

Such confession was not easy. Everybody else looked so sure and pious. But Thomas was not one to spend the rest of his life nursing unanswered questions. So, with great courage, he asked, "Where do I begin?" The question deserves an answer. You will do well to remember that *even the simplest prayer should have three parts*. Elton Trueblood has suggested that any person has made a great beginning in prayer when he sincerely utters three brief statements: "Thank you, Lord!" "Help me!" "Help John and Mary!"[1]

Start with "Thank you, Lord." (See Phil. 4:4-7.) God has given you so much! *Thanks* is one of the few things you can give him. Begin thanking God for the things he has already done in your life. Gratitude is the healthiest emotion known to mankind.

Continue with "Help me." (See Mark 11:22-25.) If you are like I am, you need all the help you can get. God cares about the things you care about. You can talk to him about everything important to you. Invite God to share the real stuff that makes up your daily life.

Confess your sins to God. Name the things you have done wrong. Tell God that you are sorry. Ask his forgiveness. Then, believe he has done what he promised: "If we confess our sins to him, he can be depended on to forgive us and to cleanse us from every wrong" (1 John 1:9, TLB.)

Finally, concentrate on the needs of others. End your prayer with "Help John and Mary." (See Jas. 5:13-16.) You may want to make a prayer list of the names of individuals you wish to remember. Be specific. Call names before God and specify their needs. It is rewarding to watch God at work in the lives of those you love. Pray for them daily.

One of the first rules for beginning pray-ers is *regularity*. Pray each day and, as much as possible, at the same time. Set a fixed time for private prayer even though you are attempting to carry on a continual conversation with God throughout the day. Pick the time best for you, and stick to it.

Matters such as time, place, format, and posture are intensely personal. The value of prayer at the beginning of the day is that God's guidance can be sought for the plans and activities of that day. We also can request God's strength for the known and unknown, the good and evil that will come to us each day.

The place of prayer should be completely private and as free as possible from interruptions. Jesus advised: "But when you pray, go to your room, close the door, and pray to your Father, who is unseen. And your Father, who sees what you do in private, will reward you" (Matt. 6:6, GNB). If you can be sure that no one will see, hear, or interrupt, you will be able to concentrate better.

There is a time to pray alone (most of the time), and a time to pray with others. Jesus both participated in and encouraged praying with a group. One of his greatest promises was not concerning the

prayer of one, but the prayer of two: " 'If two of you agree on earth about anything they ask, it will be done for them by my Father in heaven' " (Matt. 18:19, RSV).

Posture does not matter to God. It matters to us only as it reflects our attitude. Certainly all prayer cannot be with heads bowed and eyes closed. You may stand, sit, kneel, or lie down to pray. The only advantage to kneeling is that it reflects an attitude of humility. Lying down may contribute more to sleepiness than concentration.

How long should you pray? As long as praying is meaningful and helpful—and no longer. I have discovered that it is more natural for me to pray regularly and briefly than it is to indulge in long, marathon prayers one day and then skip several days. Jesus said, "But when ye pray, use not vain [empty] repetitions, as the heathen *do*: for they think that they shall be heard for their *much speaking*" (Matt. 6:7). Remember, Jesus' "Model Prayer" was only sixty-seven words long. With God, longwindedness is not a virture.

When I Don't Feel Like Praying

"What do I do when the excitement is gone?" Ron asked. "Prayer is just words. There's nobody there." Let's admit that the Christian life has good days and bad days. We all have our bouts with the spiritual blahs.

Many people, at such times, simply stop praying altogether, which is the worst possible response. This leaves God with no point of contact. Remember, the spiritual blahs, like the common cold, are neither permanent nor fatal.

You need to build some basic spiritual disciplines into your life. Prayer is one of them. The totally undisciplined life is never a live option for the Christian. We are never free from certain spiritual habits. Be honest with God. Tell him how you feel. But, you should *continue to pray whether you feel like it or not*!

Why? Because the continual Christian life is like regular eating habits. Some meals are exciting. Others are common. But we are fed.

It is better to keep in contact with God and talk with him regularly. When we pray, we can work through our problems and grow spiritually. Stay in touch with God . . . even when you don't feel like it.

CHAPTER 8

The Miracle of the Church

Memory Verse: *Acts 2:42* (card 13)

In this chapter our area of searching will be concerned with the

nature of the $\dfrac{\epsilon\kappa\kappa\lambda\eta\sigma\acute{\iota}\alpha}{\textbf{church}}$

The symbol of our search will be the spire. . . .

I BELIEVE IN AND LOVE THE CHURCH. In my search for a maturing faith, I discovered that Christ loved the church. (See Eph. 5:25.) This is a truth that makes a difference. I would like to change some things about the church; others I would like to keep. But, that doesn't disturb me.

INTERROBANG **?** It is possible to affirm our love for the church while we continue to seek change and to come to a better understanding of a complex organism.

The church is slow to change. It needs your prayers and understanding. It is good to remember that, even though a motorcycle can execute a U-turn quicker than a trailer truck, it's the truck that delivers the goods in the long run. In my own experience I have discovered that the church has spent more time waiting on me to change than I have spent waiting on it.

On the Outside—Looking In

What if you were asked to draw some conclusions about the church based entirely on the habits and practices of Christians?

A man from Mars was asked to write a research paper on "The Religion of America." Since he did not know the language, his conclusions were drawn strictly on the basis of observation. His conclusion was that Americans are sun worshippers.

The man from Mars listed numerous reasons for arriving at that conclusion. First, he noted that, one day each week, Americans by the thousands go to seashores and lakesides to worship. He observed that millions of dollars were spent annually for the equipment necessary for sun worship. By their dress and actions, the people revealed a complete submission to the god of the sun. From intensive research he discovered they met on *sun-day*.

In an attempt to be objective, the Martian felt that it was necessary to mention the existence of a peculiar sect of anti-sun worshippers. On the same day of the week they would go to buildings with stained glass windows (obviously to keep out the rays of the sun). They worshiped a little-known Jehovah God. By their dress and activities they were obviously in rebellion against the sun god. They called their meeting day "Lord's Day," in preference to sun-day. Of course, his observations were superficial—just what you would expect of a man from Mars.

What Is the Church?

That's easy, you say. The church is that red brick building at the corner of Webster and Comanche. One problem. In the New Testament the word *church* is never used to refer to a building or, for that matter, to a denomination.

If you decided to destroy your church, what would you do? What weapons would you use? Would you set fire to the building? Tear out the baptistry? Burn all the budgets? No. The New Testament concept of the church had no connection with a church building.

Others look upon the church as an institution in the community which offers certain services from time to time. It is necessary to continue official membership in order to use the facilities of the church in connection with baptism, marriage, and death. This mild form of vague religion falls far short of the New Testament concept of church.

The word *church* is used in the New Testament with a twofold meaning. In some instances it refers to the whole body of believers,

The church is never a place, but always a people; never a fold but always a flock, never a sacred building but always a believing assembly.[1]

—Anonymous

the fellowship of the redeemed everywhere, the people of God assembled or unassembled. In most cases, however, church refers to a local congregation.

The word *church* literally means the called-out ones. The church is not the building, but the believers. It is a local body of believers, banded together to carry out Christ's orders.

The risen Christ, before ascending to the Father, told us what we should be busy doing as a church: "All power is given unto me in heaven and in earth. Go ye therefore, and teach all nations, baptizing them in the name of the Father, and of the Son, and of the Holy Ghost: Teaching them to observe all things whatsoever I have commanded you: and, lo, I am with you alway, even unto the end of the world" (Matt. 28:18-20). The task of the church has never changed. We have learned quite well, however, to live with the above commands without doing them or feeling guilty about our disobedience.

Another favorite concept of *church* in the New Testament was fellowship. Paul, in writing to the Corinthian Church, closed his letter with the familiar benediction referring to "the fellowship of the Holy Spirit" (2 Cor. 13:14, RSV). This fellowship of loving concern was a product of the Spirit's presence.

A picture of this fellowship was recorded in the early chapters of Acts. Luke said of the three thousand newly baptized converts, "They joined with the other believers in regular attendance at the apostles' teaching sessions and at the Communion services and prayer meetings" (Acts 2:42, TLB). This was a twofold fellowship: (1) with God in the experience of worship, and (2) with fellow believers in a sharing of faith, a caring for one another's needs, and a bearing of one another's burdens.

When the church becomes a fellowship of loving concern, it will attract the attention of the outside world. Jesus said, "Love one another. By this shall all men know that ye are my disciples" (John 13:35). If others cannot see something beautiful in our human relationships, we are not living properly. A church that has become an unloving fellowship contradicts everything Christ taught us.

The most persuasive of all qualities is that of genuine love and concern. Unless people see in us the practice of love, they will not and should not listen when we speak to them of spiritual matters.

Would you like to become involved in a task that is of utmost importance to God? Then give your assistance in creating a fellowship of loving concern in your church. People do not rebel against the church as it is defined here. What they do rebel against is the distortion or perversion of the church as they have seen it in some unloving fellowship.

Where Is the Church on Monday?

This question presents no problem to those who go to church (meaning the building) on Sunday and give little thought to Christianity the rest of the week. For them the church is at the corner of Webster and Comanche regardless of the day of the week. But, what if the church is not the building but is the believers? What if the church is a fellowship of loving concern whether the people are assembled or unassembled? Then the question has significance: Where is the church on Monday?

The Christian life is characterized by a rhythm of come and go. Christ's commands to his followers reveal a creative tension between invitation and commission.

On one hand he invited, " 'Come to me and I will give you rest' " (Matt. 11:28, TLB). On the other hand he urged, " 'Therefore . . . make disciples of all nations' " (Matt. 28:19, RSV).

This come-and-go rhythm continues to characterize the tension in the life of the Christian. The church is to be both gathered and dispersed (scattered). There are times when we should assemble—come together; there are times when we should be scattered—go out.

On Sunday the church gathers together for the purpose of Bible study, worship, training, and prayer. These are necessary times if we wish to sustain a vital Christian experience. During these times of assembly, we come to know the Lord better; we come to a better understanding of the Christian life; and we encourage one another to be faithful. That is half the story.

Where is the church on Monday or the rest of the week? During the week the individual Christian goes out into all his world communicating the good news. Our primary ministry is not in the church, but in the world.

On Monday the church is where you are; on the job, at home with your family, in your leisure hours, at school, on the athletic field, as you take an exam, or go on a date.

The creative tension of come and go is normal in the Christian life. There is no reason to fear or resent it. The tension is a necessary part of the challenge and excitement of following Christ.

Would Jesus Go to Church?

Many people wonder if Jesus would have time for today's church. Would he attend our worship? Would he identify with the life and ministry of twentieth-century churches? Even more important, does the church deserve a place in our busy, hectic lives? The answer is important as you can see.

98

I think the answer is, "Yes." Jesus went to the Passover feast when many people thought that he wouldn't. I am convinced that Jesus would have time for today's church. We simply cannot enlist him as a detractor or minimizer of the church.

What would be his attitude toward the institution? Is it possible that Jesus would work from within to bring renewal and restoration? Because he loved the church and gave himself for it, is it too much to think that he would keep fighting for the church to mean something?

Wouldn't Jesus be able to see that the church is irrelevant? Irrelevant by whose definition? Who is qualified to recognize reality in a day when every institution in society is playing "Catch up with history"? I believe that Jesus would work for meaningful change within the church while admitting that, outside the church, there is little good news.

Would Jesus be able to put up with all the hypocrites in the church? He did when he lived on the earth. As sensitive as he was to hypocrisy, he went to the synagogue "as his custom was" on the Sabbath. Where will we go to escape hypocrites?

A hypocrite is a pretender or play-actor. He is not trying and failing. He is failing to try. This works two ways. If it is hypocritical to come to church and pretend to be something you're not, isn't it just as hypocritical to stay outside and pretend that you don't need the church, when you really do? We come to church, not because we are good, but because we are not and know we ought to be.

Would Jesus be satisfied with the dogmatism and negativism of the church? He wasn't satisfied with it before. He worked to change the legalistic, negative approach of the Pharisees. He refused to believe that people could be forced to enjoy God by forbidding them to enjoy anything else.

Jesus' entire ministry was given to show that Christianity would be more than a list of "Thou shalt not's." He stated openly that our brand of religion would have to be better than that of the Pharisees. He turned religious commitment toward the positive when he said, " 'You shall love the Lord your God with all your heart, and with all your soul, and with all your mind, and with all your strength. . . . You shall love your neighbor as yourself' " (Mark 12:30-31, RSV). Jesus insisted that no other Commandments are greater than these.

99

What About You and Your Church?

You knew this question would come sooner or later. Does the church deserve a place in *your* busy, hectic life? Will you have time for today's church? Will you attend its worship services? Will you identify with its life and ministry?

Many people have mixed feelings toward the church. Before you definitely decide that the church is wrong, consider these truths.

Jesus saw the sabbath—a day of worship—as one of God's good gifts to make life fuller and better for man. He said to the religious leaders of his day, " 'But the Sabbath was made to benefit man, and not man to benefit the Sabbath' " (Mark 2:27, TLB).

Jesus resented the inhumanity, intolerance, and over-religiousness of the Pharisees who turned the day of worship into a burden rather than a blessing. He urged his disciples not to follow their example: "Do not . . . imitate their actions, because they don't practice what they preach. They tie onto people's backs loads that are heavy and hard to carry, yet they aren't willing even to lift a finger to help them carry those loads" (Matt. 23:3-4, GNB).

Jesus encouraged a day given primarily to worship, fellowship, and rest. In this hyperactive, restless, nerve-shattering age, people need the calm, poise-restoring influence of a day of worship.

As Christians we must remember that he whom we call Lord of life is also Lord of the sabbath: " 'For I, the Messiah, am master even of the Sabbath' " (Matt. 12:8, TLB). Again he said, "So the Son of man is lord even of the sabbath" (Mark 2:28, RSV). If Jesus is Lord of our lives and Lord of the sabbath, we are directly responsible to him in our use of the day of worship.

Jesus respected the sabbath and made it a practice to attend public worship. Luke recorded: "And he came to Nazareth, where he had been brought up; and he went to the synagogue, as his custom was, on the sabbath day" (Luke 4:16, RSV).

Why did Jesus form a habit of regular attendance at public worship? After all, wasn't Nazareth a small town with ordinary people? The synagogue was a little place with worship services that probably were not particularly inspiring. The hypocrites and Pharisees were there. Legalism and negativism were as thick as peanut butter. Didn't Jesus disagree with much that was going on? Why did he keep going?

Could it be that Jesus knew the value of a time, place, and associations which make the presence of God more sure? You may ask, "But, can't we worship God anywhere?" Yes, but most of the time we don't. Most of us need the encouragement of a priceless fellowship of loving concern; a fellowship where fires are rekindled, courage is regained; and temptations are conquered.

Could it be that Jesus saw in the church a potential militant army marching off the map with the good news concerning his kingdom? If not the church, then who?

Jesus lived and died believing that ultimate victory was with the church. After Simon confessed his belief that Jesus was the Messiah, Jesus said: "Thou art Peter, and upon this rock I will build my church; and the gates of hell shall not prevail against it" (Matt. 16:18).

I am aware of the weaknesses and failures of the church. The basic problem is largely personal and spiritual. Part of the maturing process is accepting responsibility for our own failures. Perhaps it is time for you and me to admit that we are to blame for the poor showing of the church. The church's failure is our failure.

With all its faults and shortcomings, the church remains the body of Christ. Because of one bad experience, some people write off the church; they are doing the cause of Christ and themselves a great injustice. That would be like giving up baths because at one time you got into a tub and the water was too hot or too cold. It is best to keep working at it until you get the water just right.

I urge you to stay with the church. Keep fighting and praying for the church to mean something. Help bring about the necessary changes. Instead of kicking on the outside, work on the inside.

The church will help you avoid two extremes: an isolation from the world which would result in a "holier-than-thou" attitude and an imitation of the world which would result in a "worldier-than-thou" attitude.

Why Do We Need the Church?

One of the great discoveries of the twentieth century has been the recognition of the necessity of the church in any vital Christianity. The church is not optional for the believer.

We need the church, because *it constantly confronts the non-*

Christian world with the claims of Christ. The risen Christ commissioned his church to do three things: (1) make disciples in all nations, (2) baptize them, and (3) teach them to obey all his commands. (See Matt. 28:19-20.) The work of the church is not complete until these three important matters are accomplished for every person.

The church is uniquely qualified to carry out this Commission—not in part but in full. In recent years many small groups have developed outside the church, and compete for the attention of the people. It is not a question of whether these groups are good or bad. Most people are blessed by these small groups during some critical years of their Christian experience.

Before a person allows these groups to become substitutes for his church, he should ask some further questions: Is this group carrying out the Great Commission of Christ: Is this group interested in training the new convert as well as winning him? Will this group minister to my spiritual needs the rest of my life, or is it limited to a few years? Is this group interested in baptizing the new convert as Christ commands? If any of these questions receive a negative answer, the group will never be a worthy substitute for the church.

We need the church because *it provides the fellowship and resources necessary for Christian growth.* You and I need all the help we can get to live the Christian life. In the church we keep an eye on one another. We watch after one another. We encourage one another in the improvement of our weaknesses. We praise one another because of our strengths. We stimulate one another to noble living. We provide a fellowship of acceptance that gives even the outsider a sense of belonging. This is the church at its best.

The book of Acts contains a beautiful glimpse of the ministry of the early church. On Paul's first missionary journey stones were hurled at him outside Lystra, and he was left for dead: "As the disciples stood round about him, he rose up, and came into the city" (Acts 14:20). The world had done what it could do to silence Paul. They walked away satisfied with a job well-done. Then the disciples came and formed a circle around him. They nursed his wounds. They gave him strength and encouragement. They put fresh heart and determination into him. Finally, on his own

The Church has many critics but no rivals.[3]   —Anonymous

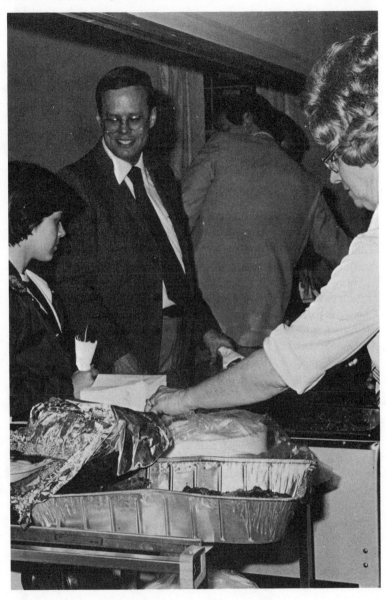

strength, he went back into the same city. The ministry of the church is to form a circle of love and concern around all believers in their times of need.

As Christians, we need one another. We need the strength, comfort, encouragement, and stimulation to noble living that comes from the fellowship of the church. The writer of Hebrews issued a challenge and a warning to every believer: "Let us consider how to stir up one another to love and good works, not neglecting to meet together, as is the habit of some, but encouraging one another, and all the more as you see the Day drawing near" (Heb. 10:24-25, RSV).

The writing of the New Testament was not complete, and some believers had already formed the habit of not attending public worship. William Barclay warned, "There is no man who can live the Christian life and neglect the fellowship of the Church."[2] You may disagree with this statement. I have watched many Christians attempt to disprove it. Most of them became hopelessly cold and indifferent to spiritual things.

There is no more effective denial of all Christ means than to cut oneself from the fellowship of believers. Generally, when the Christian neglects worship, spiritual growth stops. He begins to live for trifles, and the light of hope leaves his eyes.

We need the church because *it is the most effective deterrent to our going back to old ways*. A constant possibility facing every Christian is that his heart will turn away from God and back to those things which characterized his life before he became a Christian. When this happens, the major causes will be spiritual loneliness and the neglect of spiritual resources.

We need the mutual encouragement we receive within the fellowship of the church: "But encourage one another day after day, as long as it is still called 'Today,' lest any one of you be hardened by the deceitfulness of sin" (Heb. 3:13, NASB).

A church can well afford to lose almost anything rather than lose its fellowship of mutual encouragement.

The Miracle of the Church

It looks as though the church will be around for awhile. If the church were going to be destroyed by external criticism or to commit suicide by internal indifference, it would have happened long ago. You and I are confronted constantly with the miracle of the church.

Periodically, I visit with people who have either given up on the church or consider that God has passed it by. They seem to feel sorry for me, because my life is committed to an institution that is on the way out. Then I remember the words of Jesus: "Upon this rock I will build my church; and the gates of hell shall not prevail against it" (Matt. 16:18). I begin to look around at my alternatives. Is there an organization outside the church that has the stamp of God's approval? Has God provided us a substitute for the church? When I compare the outside possibilities to what the church could be if it really came alive, my decision is to stay with the church and work for its renewal.

The church has survived the neglect and indifference of the majority of its members. Nothing but a divine institution under the direct blessing of God could have survived the shallow, superficial commitment of so many people. The miracle of the church is that it survives!

The church not only survives, it also contains the greatest number of people committed to God to be found anywhere. Where else would you go to find a greater number of potential recruits for what God wishes to do in today's world?

I urge you to stay close to the church. That's where the action is! What happens to and in the church is supremely important in today's world. And, what happens in the world will depend largely on what first happens in your church.

The greatest miracle of all is that the church is open to all kinds of people. The church is more a "sinners' anonymous" than a "saints' conservatory." We must never forget that "Whosoever will may come."

Honestly Now

What kind of church member are you? List some ways in which your church could be improved. Beside each item, write how you can help your church to be better in each area.

CHAPTER 9

The Ordinances: Baptism and the Lord's Supper

Memory Verses: *Romans 6:4; 1 Corinthians 11:26* (cards 14-15)

Thousands of years from now when archaeologists uncover a Baptist church, regardless of its size or geographical location, they will find that two things probably occupied places of importance. One will be a modern convenience called a baptistry—a watertight tank large enough for complete immersion. The other will be a table, located front and center, from which the Lord's Supper was served, with the words *In Remembrance of Me* inscribed on it.

These two props form a backdrop for a symbolic drama of Christianity. The New Testament church had two ordinances: baptism and the Lord's Supper. The drama has two acts. Each act reveals things worth remembering about the life, ministry, death, and resurrection of Jesus Christ.

The word *ordinance* means a decree or command—something ordained by Christ. Baptism and the Lord's Supper are symbolic acts commanded by Jesus to signify what he did to make our salvation possible. (Read Matt. 28:19; Luke 22:19; 1 Cor. 11:23-26.)

The purpose of this chapter is to explore the meaning of these aids to our practice of the Christian faith. The two ordinances strengthen the memory by adding sight and taste to hearing. The cup and the bread will serve as our symbol.

The two ordinances symbolize some important truths of the Christian gospel. Interpreting them in the light of these New Testament truths is essential to our understanding why we as Baptists observe the ordinances.

The Ordinance of Baptism

"Why all the fuss about baptism?" Mark wanted to know. "Haven't I heard you say that baptism isn't necessary to salvation? If baptism doesn't help save us, then why is so much emphasis placed on it when a person wants to join the church?" Many young people struggle with this question.

The answer is in chronology—the order in which things happen. Two questions are important: (1) How does an individual become a Christian? (2) What should a person do after he becomes a Christian? Baptism comes into the picture only when we discuss the second question.

It is true that baptism does not save. Nor does it complete one's salvation. At the same time, every believer must take baptism seriously for three reasons: (1) because Jesus himself was baptized, (2) because Jesus placed his stamp of approval on the baptismal activity of his disciples, and (3) because he commissioned his followers to baptize new converts. What about Jesus? Was he baptized? Yes, he was. "Then Jesus went from Galilee to the Jordan River to be baptized there by John. John didn't want to do it.

'This isn't proper,' he said. 'I am the one who needs to be baptized by you.'

But Jesus said, 'Please do it, for I must do all that is right.' So then John baptized him" (Matt. 3:13-15, TLB).

By submitting to John's baptism, Jesus placed his stamp of approval on John's ministry, set an example for all his followers, and dedicated himself publicly to a redemptive ministry. In baptism he symbolized his death, burial, and resurrection.

In John 4:1-2, we read of a time when greater crowds came to Jesus than to John to be baptized. A note of explanation was added: "Jesus himself baptized not, but his disciples." Apparently Jesus agreed to this practice of baptism.

At the close of his physical ministry, the risen Christ gave his "marching orders" to the New Testament church. His instructions were to go and make disciples of all nations, "baptizing them in the name of the Father, and of the Son, and of the Holy Ghost" (Matt. 28:19).

What Is the Purpose of Baptism?

Because baptism is symbolic in nature and not sacramental (does not impart grace), the next consideration must be its purpose or meaning. What does baptism symbolize? What are the "things worth remembering" that are constantly called to mind by this symbolic drama?

First of all, baptism points back in time to the death, burial, and resurrection of Jesus. Each baptism is a commemoration of these central affirmations of the Christian faith. Baptism symbolizes a salvation that comes by faith in Christ.

A second purpose of baptism is to dramatize the present experience of the believer. Baptism symbolizes death to sin, burial with Christ, and resurrection to walk a new life with him. Paul described it beautifully: "We were buried therefore with him by baptism into death, so that as Christ was raised from the dead by the glory of the Father, we too might walk in newness of life" (Rom. 6:4, RSV).

Baptism may be considered a part of the new convert's public testimony of faith in Christ. When he walks down into the baptismal waters, he is saying, "I have died to an old, sinful way of life." When he is placed beneath the water, he is saying, "I am being buried to the old way of life." Then, as he is raised out of the water, he is saying, "I am being raised to walk in a completely new life with Christ."

Baptism, then, is an outward symbol of an inward experience. Unless the person being baptized has had the inner experience, baptism is robbed of its meaning. For that reason, throughout their history Baptists have baptized believers only.

In this respect, baptism may be compared to a marriage ceremony. Taking marriage vows does not *cause* two people to fall in love. The wedding ceremony is assumed to be an outward sign or symbol of an inner love and commitment which already exists.

108

What Is the Mode of Baptism?

Baptists did not choose their name. In the seventeenth century those who insisted on the immersion of believers only were branded Anabaptists (rebaptizers). In an effort to shun that name, they began calling themselves Baptized churches. Toward the close of the eighteenth century, the descriptive adjective *baptized* was modified and shortened in popular usage to *Baptist*, which became the accepted title.

As you might expect, the people called *Baptists* had some strong convictions about baptism. Two of these convictions emerged early and remain at the heart of Baptist teachings: (1) insistence upon the baptism of believers only, and (2) baptism by immersion only. Our present concern is with the second conviction—that immersion constitutes the act of baptism.

Why do Baptists continue to insist upon immersion? Isn't it true that many church groups are now sprinkling and pouring as modes of baptism? Wouldn't those methods be less expensive and more convenient? The answer to the last two questions is *yes*. Now, let me attempt an answer to the first question. Basically there are three reasons why Baptists have continued to practice immersion.

The first reason has to do with the meaning of the Greek word used for baptism in the New Testament. The word *baptizo* means to dip, plunge, submerge, or immerse. Most Christian scholars agree that New Testament baptism was by immersion. Classical Greek used the word *baptizo* to describe a ship sinking into the sea.

A second reason is that the description of baptism, as practiced in New Testament times, suggested immersion. The Gospel of Mark carries this account of the baptism of Jesus by John in the Jordan river: "He went up immediately from the water, and behold, the heavens were opened" (1:10, RSV). Also, the record of Philip baptizing the eunuch was a clear description of immersion: "They both went down into the water, . . . and he baptized him. And when they came up out of the water, the Spirit of the Lord caught up Philip; and the eunuch saw him no more, and went on his way rejoicing" (Acts 8:38-39, RSV).

The final reason Baptists insist on immersion is a logical one having to do with the meaning of the symbolism. What is baptism intended to symbolize? We already have concluded that it symbolizes death, burial, and resurrection. (See Rom. 6:2-4.) Only immersion fully accomplishes this symbolism.

Generally it is agreed that immersion was the original form of baptism. Baptists have felt that it is impossible to change the mode without changing the meaning. For that reason we have continued to immerse those who come for membership in our churches.

Who Should Be Baptized?

Do you remember how we got our name? We are called *Baptists* because we have some strong convictions about baptism. One of these—that baptism should be by immersion only—we have already discussed. Now we are ready to examine another conviction—our insistence on *the baptism of believers only*.

Careful study shows that believers' baptism was the only kind of baptism practiced in New Testament times. A certain order repeated itself: (1) an individual heard the gospel, (2) accepted its message, (3) believed in Christ as his Savior, and (4) was baptized. The chronology of the Great Commission is important: first we are to "make disciples," next we are to "baptize them," then they must be "taught" how to live the Christian life. (See Matt. 28:19-20.) Believers are the only proper subjects for baptism.

John the Baptist demanded fruits worthy of repentance before he would baptize those who came to him. He said, " 'Before being baptized, prove that you have turned from sin by doing worthy deeds' " (Matt. 3:8, TLB). On the day of Pentecost those who "gladly received his word" were baptized (Acts 2:41). According to the New Testament pattern, baptism is the believer's first opportunity to proclaim his faith in Christ.

Again, baptism is an outward symbol of an inward experience. The inward experience is one of death and burial to an old way of life and resurrection to newness of life. Unless the person being baptized can testify to this experience, baptism is robbed of its meaning.

For this reason, Baptists do not practice infant baptism. Because infants are not in the position to have a personal faith in Christ, any baptism performed in their behalf cannot express the meaning of Christian baptism.

Some people believe that the child is born condemned and that

110

baptism results in salvation for the infant. Others believe that the child from birth is in the kingdom and that baptism and Christian training simply keep the child in the kingdom. Baptists believe that the new-born infant is kept under the protective grace of God until he reaches an age of accountability or responsibility. At such time, the child can decide for himself to be a follower of Christ. When he is old enough to decide for himself, he is also old enough to be baptized by immersion. Then, his baptism can express the full meaning and intended symbolism.

Would you like to wade out into deeper waters? Read Acts 19:1-5. What is the difference between John's baptism and Christian baptism? Is a second immersion ever necessary? or logical? If so, under what circumstances?

One Other Question

What about an immersion performed by some other denomination? Is it true that some Baptist churches ask certain people to be immersed again?

You will find different practices among Baptist churches at this point. Some churches receive persons with such baptisms, while others do not. Each congregation is autonomous (not told what to do by any other group or any other person). It is free to decide and it is also responsible for its decisions. Those who accept these baptisms generally do so only after careful study to be sure that the proper motive, meaning, purpose, and symbolism have been preserved.

Those who reject such baptisms do so for a variety of reasons. A person's baptism generally is not accepted when it was performed for its sacramental value (immersion *for* salvation). Also, a baptism might be rejected—even when immersion is the mode—if it was performed by a group which does not stress believers' baptism.

When a second immersion is requested, it is generally to accomplish one or all of three things: (1) Because Baptists believe that baptism is a part of a person's public profession of faith, at times we may ask that this confession be made before a new body of baptized believers. (2) We also may ask that a person's baptism show a willing commitment to a new body of beliefs. (3) We desire that all who come into membership in Baptist churches do so out of serious commitment and conviction.

The Ordinance of the Lord's Supper

The second act in the church's "symbolic drama" of Christianity is the Lord's Supper. Its purpose is to reveal some "things worth remembering" about the death of Christ for a world's sin. The Lord's Supper is a powerful aid to Christian memory because it adds sight and taste to hearing.

The observance of the Lord's Supper was instituted at the end of Jesus' earthly ministry. He and his disciples had gathered in Jerusalem to share the Passover feast. Jesus knew that this would be their last meal together. What could he say or do on this occasion to leave his followers a continuing reminder of his love and willing sacrifice? He invited them to share in a memorial supper. (See Matt. 26:26-30). Unfortunately, this ordinance has been the subject of much controversy as to its meaning and its observance.

The Four Historic Views

Christian history reveals four distinct views concerning the meaning of the Lord's Supper.

1. *Roman Catholics* believe that, when the priest consecrates the bread and wine, they are actually changed into the substance of the flesh and blood of Christ (*transubstantiation*). Although the appearance and taste remain the same, those who partake are eating the flesh and drinking the blood of Christ.

2. *Lutherans* deny the change of substance while affirming that Christ is bodily present "in, with, and under" the substance of bread and wine (*consubstantiation*). Martin Luther insisted on a literal interpretation of the words "This is my body" and "This is my blood."

3. *Calvinistic* theology insists that Christ is not bodily present, but is spiritually present in the elements of bread and wine. This spiritual presence, however, is different from any other spiritual

112

presence of Jesus. In other words, a definite spiritual blessing (grace) comes to the believer in the observance of the Lord's Supper—a grace which is not available otherwise.

These three views have one thing in common; each is considered to be a means of receiving grace. They contribute to an individual's salvation. Persons who hold these views believe that blessings come to the believer during the Lord's Supper which can be received through no other experience.

4. The Lord's Supper has a *symbolic meaning* (*Zwinglian*). Historically, Baptists have been identified with this fourth view. This beautiful ordinance is strictly a memorial supper. The bread and the fruit of the vine are symbols of the broken body and spilled blood of Jesus.

Baptists believe that, when Jesus said, "This is my body," and, "This is my blood," he was speaking symbolically—not literally. He was saying that the bread and the fruit of the vine represent, picture, or symbolize his body and blood. They become visual aids portraying that which Jesus did for man's salvation.

Does this mean that Baptists deny the spiritual presence of Christ in the Lord's Supper? Not at all. We believe that his presence here is not different from his constant presence in the life of every believer or his presence any other place in the universe. Do Baptists deny that the Lord's Supper can be a special blessing for the believer? Certainly not. What we deny is that grace is given— that a person is "more a Christian" for having participated.

What Is the Meaning of the Lord's Supper?

Because the Lord's Supper is symbolic in its significance, the main emphasis for the believer is commemoration. This means it is a reminder of what Jesus did for us.

To make the most of the observance requires preparation and personal effort. Many Christians have discovered new meaning in the Lord's Supper by considering the various dimensions of its message.

Jesus instituted the Supper to preserve for all future Christians an authentic memory of his sufferings. This is *the backward look* of the Supper (1 Cor. 11:26). It receives its meaning from the past. Apart from the past deed—Christ's death on the cross—the present memorial would be emptied of its meaning. While observing the Supper, remember "I have been died for, and by the Son of God, at that!"

The Lord's Supper also provides an excellent opportunity for *an inward look*. Paul admonished, "But let a man examine himself and so let him eat of that bread, and drink of that cup" (1 Cor. 11:28). Celebration and confession go well together.

In the Lord's Supper observance, the believer *looks forward* with hope: "For as often as ye eat this bread, and drink this cup, ye do shew the Lord's death *till he come*" (1 Cor. 11:26). We gain assurance from the promise of Christ's return and the knowledge that he is the ultimate Victor.

The Lord's Supper is an ordinance of the church. Its meaning, therefore, would be incomplete without *the outward look*. We not only enjoy communion with Christ, but also communion with one another as believers. It is a constant reminder that we are not alone, but a part of a larger body of believers who also are trying to grow toward maturity in the Christian faith.

Who Should Participate?

Because the Lord's Supper is a church ordinance and not taken individually, the church must accept the responsibility for its administration. For example, the individual church determines how often the Supper is observed. Specific instructions are not given in the New Testament. Paul's only advice was that as often as we do observe it, it should be done in remembrance of Christ (1 Cor. 11:25).

The same is true in discussing who should participate. Every denomination and each church has its own set of qualifications and restrictions.

Among all Christian groups there is general agreement that some restrictions are necessary. The invitation to the Lord's Table is not to all the world. Certainly it would be limited to Christians; otherwise it loses its significance. There would be no meaning in inviting non-Christians to an observance celebrating the event that founded Christianity. The question is, How restricted shall it be?

Historically, an impressive number of Baptist churches practiced what is called "closed communion." This view holds that a person should be a member of the church in which he partakes of the Supper. The idea here is that the participant should be in the fellowship and under the discipline of the church which offers the Supper.

Many Baptist churches, however, agree that any member of any Baptist church is eligible. Herschel H. Hobbs in *The Baptist Faith and Message* has written, "New Testament baptized believers are eligible to take the Lord's Supper." In this case the Supper would be restricted to those who are believers and have been baptized according to the New Testament pattern of immersion. Some Baptist churches, in embracing this view, would not require membership in a Baptist church before participation in the Supper.

Again, each congregation is an autonomous unit. You will find different practices among Baptist churches. The final decision must be made by the church. Regardless of the view, the Lord's Supper should be presented in a loving and worshipful manner.

And Now, in Conclusion . . .

Why did Jesus institute these ordinances? Because the heart of the gospel is set forth in their observance. They are sermons in symbols. Baptism reminds us of the death, burial, and resurrection of Jesus. It is an initial act, administered at the beginning of the Christian experience. The Lord's Supper helps us remember the sacrifice of Jesus on the cross. It is a continuing reminder, observed throughout the Christian's life.

Both ordinances are commanded by Jesus. They are respected, followed, and cherished by believers. No magic or saving power is contained within them. Any change must take place in the heart— not in the baptismal water or in the elements of the Lord's Supper.

Chapter 10

First Things About Last Things—a Theology of Christian Hope

Memory Verse: *John 14:3* (card 16)

With regard to the future of the world, most people fit into one of three groups: (1) those who are so concerned with the present that they seldom think about the future, (2) those who seldom think about anything else, and (3) those who are prepared to face their deaths and are content to leave the time and details to God.

At one time or another, most people wonder about the future of the world. This may be caused by a deepening pessimism about world conditions. When a person views the world as sitting on a powder keg and inhabited by idiots with hands full of matches, he has little hope.

Where is our hope? Is the human drama moving toward the final scene? Is history going somewhere or nowhere? Will goodness or nothingness prevail? What do *you* think about the future?

Eschatology (*the study of last things*) is best understood as a part of the overall kingdom of God. The kingdom had a *beginning*. Jesus initiated it when he came and established the rule of God in the hearts of men. The kingdom also *is a continuing process*. The work Jesus began continues as a spiritual experience and a present reality. Paul wrote, "And I am sure that he who began a good work in you will bring it to completion at the day of Jesus Christ (Phil. 1:6, RSV). The *final stage* of the kingdom is the eternal kingdom to be ushered in at the second coming of Christ. He will not leave unfinished what he has begun. In his first coming he made the "down payment," and he will come again to claim those who are his.

As Christians, we believe this world had a definite beginning, and in the purpose of God it is moving toward a fitting conclusion. In his own time the author of the drama will come down to the earth's stage and will announce to humanity, "Gentlemen, it's closing time." The study of the end of the world we call eschatology (*eschatos* means "last," and *logos* means "word" or "doctrine"). This chapter will present the teachings about "last things."

έσχατος + λογός

Eschatology

No one symbol is adequate. Perhaps this cluster of symbols will have meaning for you as you proceed.

Is Death to Be Feared?

Fear of death is not unusual, even among Christians. We tend to fear anything that is unknown. At best, death remains a mystery. For most people it is a crisis which involves both major and minor changes. On the subject of death, most of us would prefer to be silent. Yet, as Christians, the very least we can do is face the fact that death is a reality.

The Bible takes death seriously. In the Old Testament, death and the future life are generally presented in dark and gloomy terms. Even though death is not regarded as the "end of it all," the Old Testament does not give much light on life beyond the grave. Death is referred to as the "king of terrors" (Job 18:14).

In the New Testament, the most common word used for death (*thanatos*) means a separation. In other words, when the spirit dwells in the physical body, there is physical life. When the spirit is separated from the body, the body is dead. Death also implies separation from the world of living persons. That is physical death.

The New Testament also speaks of "spiritual death" as the separation of the soul from God (Eph. 2:1; Col. 2:13). The mystery of death is intensified when we realize that a person might be dead

117

spiritually while still alive physically—and he may continue to live spiritually after he has died physically.

The concept of death is completely transformed in the New Testament. The Old Testament darkness and gloom became light and hope. Jesus referred to death as sleep (Mark 5:39), and said, "Whosoever liveth and believeth in me shall never die" (John 11:26). His own resurrection from the dead transformed our concept of death. We cherish his promise: "Because I live, ye shall live also" (John 14:19). This makes possible Paul's triumphant shout of faith, "For to me to live is Christ, and to die is gain" (Phil. 1:21).

What is the Christian view of death? Death is not punishment handed out by God, so much as it is an unavoidable consequence of man's behavior. The world which God created was good. His original order was necessary to life. Man's disobedience and claim to be his own god disturbed the order of perfection. The world in which we live is "out of order." Death is a natural part of life. Death is not a threat; it is a warning. God is God when we live. God is God when we die.

For the Christian, death is not a dead-end street; it is a thoroughfare. Death is not the end of the drama; it is the end of the first act. Death is not a termination point; it is a gateway into eternal life. Death is understood fully only in the light of resurrection. The other side of the cross is an empty tomb. "To be continued" might well be written on every gravestone.

What Does Resurrection Mean?

Job asked, "If a man die, shall he live again?" (Job 14:14). The clearest answer was given by Jesus when he affirmed the fact of the resurrection. (Read Matt. 8:11; 22:23-33.)

Jesus' faith in the resurrection was grounded in what he believed about the nature of God. He said, "He is not the God of the dead, but the God of the living" (Mark 12:27). God is not only the God of the living, but he is also the living God. He is the God of today and the God of tomorrow. He is the God of what is and what is yet to be.

As Jesus approached the day of his own death, he talked with Martha of Bethany, one of his closest friends. He shared with her an affirmation that has become central to the Christian faith: " 'I am the resurrection and the life; he who believes in me, though he die, yet shall he live, and whoever lives and believes in me shall never die' " (John 11:25-26, RSV).

As Christians we believe that the dead shall be raised. The word translated resurrection (*anastasis*) means "a raising up" or "to stand again." It refers to something dead which is made to live again. For believers in Christ, the grave is not the end. Life is more than defeat by death. We believe in resurrection because we believe that Christ was raised from the dead. Take the resurrection hope from Christianity and you leave the gospel without listeners.

What will this new life be like? Paul sought for an illustration that would help us see that the new life would be similar, yet different. (See 1 Cor. 15:1-58.) He wrote to the Corinthians about the seed that is put in the ground and out of it grows a plant. The plant is not the same as the seed, yet it contains the same life that was in the seed.

In the same way the physical body is returned to the earth, and out of the old body comes a new one—a spiritual body—with higher powers, and yet it is continuous with the old. (See 1 Cor. 15:42-49.)

Paul confessed that this transformation was "a great mystery" (v. 51). Yet, it remains the Christian's foundation of faith and hope.

First Things About the Second Coming

Jesus is coming again. We have assurance that Christ will not leave unfinished what he has begun. The concept that Christ will make one final appearance at the end of the world "fits in" with the biblical perspective concerning history (Matt. 25:31; Titus 2:13). A vital part of our Christian hope is our belief in a divine event toward which the whole creation moves.

This expected appearance of Christ is called "the second coming." The New Testament word used to describe it is *parousia*, and means "presence" or "advent." Care must be taken to avoid two extremes: (1) ignore it, hoping it will go away or (2) overemphasize it, giving attention to details known only to God.

My purpose is to relate *what we can know* from clear New Testament teachings. It is not the purpose of this brief work to deal with the differences in interpretation of the details.

One thing we know about the second coming is *its certainty*. The fact of Jesus' return to the earth at the end of history is a central part of the biblical message. Christ himself left us the promise: " 'Let not your heart be troubled: ... I go to prepare a place for you. And if I go and prepare a place for you, I *will come again*, and receive you unto myself; that where I am, there ye may be also" (John 14:1-3).

Early in the book of Acts it is recorded that Jesus ascended into the sky while witnesses stared after him. "As they were straining their eyes for another glimpse, suddenly two white-robed men were standing there among them, and said, 'Men of Galilee, why are you standing here staring at the sky? Jesus has gone away to heaven, and *some day*, just as he went, *he will return!*' " (Acts 1:10-11, TLB). The New Testament abounds in such promises.

We do not know when the second coming will occur. Jesus himself did not know: "But of that day and hour knoweth no man, no, not the angels of heaven, but my Father only" (Matt. 24:36). He warned, "Be on the alert, for you do not know which day your Lord is coming" (Matt. 24:42, NASB). Men are to be ready constantly: "For in such an hour as ye think not the Son of man cometh" (Matt. 24:44). His coming will be as a thief in the night (Matt. 24:43).

All these references point to the fact that Jesus' coming will be sudden, mysterious, and unexpected. Yet, few things have consumed so much Christian energy across the centuries as trying to pinpoint the actual time. Sometimes, people take Jesus at his word when he promises to come again, and then ignore his words about the uncertainty of the time in history.

To be curious about the future is easier than to be faithful in the present. This happened in Thessalonica not twenty years after Jesus died. Some of the people were so caught up in the immediate return of the Lord that they quit their jobs and became idle busybodies who sat around discussing the future. Paul rebuked them and commanded them to do their work in quietness, to earn their own living, and not to be weary in well-doing (2 Thess. 3:10-13).

Jesus specifically has given us our responsibility concerning his return. He cautioned, "Therefore be ye also ready: for in such an hour as ye think not the Son of man cometh" (Matt. 24:44). It helps to remember that Jesus has appointed us to the Preparations Committee—not time, place, and program. He calls for each of us to bring our lives into right relationship with God. Then we are to give our energies to living the kinds of lives that will prepare us to meet him without shame.

Neither Jesus nor his inspired writers gave us a detailed and ordered account of the events related to his second coming. It is enough to know that Christ will return. We can leave the details to him. When the condition is right in God's judgment, that will be the time of the Lord's return.

And Then Comes Judgment

People today find it difficult to believe that, sooner or later, they must sit at the judgment of results and consequences. Paul warned: "Be not deceived; God is not mocked: for whatsoever a man soweth, that shall he also reap. For he that soweth to his flesh shall of the flesh reap corruption; but he that soweth to the Spirit shall of the Spirit reap life everlasting" (Gal. 6:7-8). These verses present both the law of identical harvest and the law of personal development—you reap what you sow. If the lower nature dominates, you may expect a harvest of trouble. If the higher nature dominates, you may expect an abundant life.

The principle of judgment in God's dealings with man runs all the way through history, human experience, and the Bible. Because man is created in the image of God and has moral freedom, he is also responsible to God. In a sermon preached on Mars' Hill, Paul warned the Athenians: "And the times of this ignorance God winked at; but now commandeth all men everywhere to repent: Because he hath appointed a day, in the which he will judge the world in righteousness" (Acts 17:30-31). In Hebrews 9:27, the same truth has been stressed: "And as it is appointed unto men once to die, but after this judgment."

When will judgment be? Certainly at the time God has appointed. Other Scripture places it after the resurrection (Matt. 12:41-42) and at the time of the second coming of Christ (Matt. 24:40-42). Judgment will mark the end of our present world order and the beginning of an eternal order.

What is the purpose of the judgment? Obviously it is not to

begin an investigation to determine whether the individual is saved or lost. Man has already determined that by his decision about Christ, made during his lifetime. Besides, the God of infinite wisdom needs no such court of investigation.

Judgment will bring to light each man's character and the total effect of his influence on others. Judgment does not decide or determine an individual's destiny. Character determines destiny. Judgment merely will assign a destiny in accordance with the person's character.

The judgment will bring the affairs of human history to a completion and, at that time, an eternal order will be initiated. The saved will be glorified because of their faith and rewarded according to their works. The unsaved will be condemned because of their unbelief and sentenced according to their works.

Judgment is never understood apart from man's responsibility to God. As Christians, we believe that we live in a world created by God. As free moral agents, we are free to choose or reject God. We are accountable, therefore, to him for our lives. "In him we live, and move, and have our being" (Acts 17:28).

Becoming a Christian does not deliver us from responsibility; it increases our accountability. "To blame or to repent," that is the question. To blame others is to deny personal responsibility. To repent is to accept responsibility and move toward reconciliation.

Is There a Heaven and a Hell?

The final phase of our study of last things must introduce the subject of eternal destiny. Is there some way to outlive death? If so, what does eternity mean? Is there really a place of punishment called hell? What will heaven be like? There are too many questions and too little space to answer. Hold tight. The pace from here is breathtaking.

Heaven is God's eternal home where love is supreme. You will notice that Bible teachings about heaven are restrained. The Bible tells us all we need to know, but it may not tell us all we wish to know. We are told that, after the resurrection and judgment, the righteous will enter the eternal state called "heaven."

Jesus gave a description of heaven which satisfies most believers. He said, "In my Father's house are many mansions [dwelling-

122

places]" (John 14:2). First of all, heaven is his Father's house or home. Jesus was going home—a place of security, a place where an individual can grow and share, and above all, a place of love. And there are many rooms in that home. Everyone will have his place. There will be no space problems.

Jesus further stated, "I go to prepare a place for you" (v. 2). Heaven is a prepared place for prepared people. It is a locality and not merely a state of being. Where Jesus was going to make ready living space for his followers was home.

Finally Jesus said, "That where I am, there ye may be also" (v. 3). "Where I am" is perhaps our best description of heaven—it is where Jesus is!

Heaven will be a place of freedom from those things which make life hard: sorrow, tears, pain, and death (Rev. 21:4). It also will be a place of rewards for faithful service (Matt. 25:14-30; Luke 19:12-27). In heaven we will enjoy perfect fellowship with Christ. It is a place where we may express endless gratitude (Rev. 5:9-12) and experience endless growth. With all hindrances removed, we shall go on growing in grace and serving with joy (Rev. 22:3).

Hell may be described as the opposite of heaven. Heaven is to be at home with God. Hell is separation from God. It is where response to God is no longer possible, where love and fellowship with the Father are absent. Many people deny the reality of hell. Yet Jesus said more about hell than he did about heaven. To wish there were no hell does not change the reality. The Bible teaches that, after the resurrection and judgment, the wicked enter the eternal state of punishment called *hell*.

The ideas of divine judgment and punishment for sin are inseparable. We already have established man's accountability before God. Sin and punishment also are inseparable. To say that a merciful God would not allow hell is to examine only one facet of God's nature. God is also just. If the wicked and righteous are to be treated alike, where is the justice of God? Besides, God does not send men to hell. They go there in spite of all God has done to prevent it.

The New Testament uses two different words for the English word *hell*. The first is the word *Hades* which refers to the grave or the abode of the dead without respect to moral conditions (Matt.

11:23; 16:18; Luke 16:23; Rev. 1:18). The second is the word *Gehenna* which actually denotes a place of punishment. It is the Greek name for the Valley of Hinnom located south and east of Jerusalem. At one time, human sacrifices had been offered there (2 Kings 23:10). Later, it became Jerusalem's garbage dump. Fires burned continually to destroy the loathsome refuse of the city. The name of this local place, *Gehenna,* became the descriptive name for the place of eternal separation and punishment for those who choose not to know God (Rom. 1:28). Heaven is the eternal home of those who know Christ; and hell, the eternal abode of those who reject him.

Conclusion: How to Live Before Christ's Coming

We spend most of our lives living "in the meantime"—waiting on significant events to happen. For two thousand years Christians have lived in-between Christ's first coming and his second coming. We still face the difficult task of living in the in-between time. Our responsibility is to take the biblical teachings concerning the "last things" and apply them to the here and now.

Peter gave Christians clear instructions as to "what manner of persons" they ought to be in light of the second coming, "What sort of persons ought you to be in lives of holiness and godliness" (2 Pet. 3:11, RSV). "Dear friends," he continued, "while you are waiting for these things to happen and for him to come, try hard to live without sinning; and be at peace with everyone so that he will be pleased with you when he returns" (v. 14, TLB).

Do you know why Jesus delays his return? He has a definite purpose: "And count the forbearance of our Lord as salvation" (2 Pet. 3:15, RSV). Peter also said, "The Lord is not slow about his promise as some count slowness, but is forbearing toward you, not wishing that any should perish, but that all should reach repentance" (2 Pet. 3:9, RSV).

Today, God calls Christians to lives of holiness and godliness. He calls those who are not Christians to repent and turn to him.

Personal Learning Activities

Chapter 1
1. Complete the activities on pages 9 and 15.
2. Read slowly 1 John 4:7-21. Imagine that you are reading these verses for the very first time. What questions/feelings enter your mind?
3. Write the letter to God on page 23.
4. Memorize Scripture Memory Cards 1-3.

Chapter 2
1. Complete the response activity on page 25.
2. Define incarnation.
3. Was Jesus *not able* to sin or *able not* to sin? Explain your answer.
4. Complete the response activity "Honestly Now" on page 36.
5. Memorize Scripture Memory Cards 4 and 5.

Chapter 3
1. In light of John 14:15-18, where is Jesus today?
2. How is the concept of the Trinity meaningful to you?
3. How can the Holy Spirit help you? Give Scripture references to support your answers.
4. Unscramble the following phrases to find out who the Holy Spirit is and what he does.

Scrambled Word Puzzle
a. nidive lunrocose (John 14:16)
b. apnetrenm tdsireen (John 14:17)
c. larpones eearhct (John 14:26)
d. sevoinccn bnlveeeiur of ins (John 16:8)
e. templorec of tCisrh's ginnairt (John 16:12-15)
f. orlepnas ewpro (Acts 1:8)

g. selosdnb in etinsws (Acts 1:8)
(See p. 139 for answers.)

5. Memorize Scripture Memory Cards 6 and 7.

Chapter 4

1. Complete the response activity on page 50.
2. Paraphrase Psalm 8.
3. Complete the response activity "Honestly Now" on page 59.
4. Check statements with which you agree.

What Is a Person?

_____ A person is a highly developed animal.

_____ A person has a conscience.

_____ A person can sacrifice.

_____ A person is an entity unto himself.

_____ A person can worship.

_____ A person is only a part of the system with mainly economic value.

_____ A person is godlike.

_____ A person is a finished product.

_____ A person is continually in creation.

_____ A person is made to serve society.

_____ A person is essentially evil.

_____ A person is made for pleasure.

_____ A person is dependent on God.

_____ A person is made for work.

_____ A person is made to serve God.

_____ A person is made to love.

_____ A person can reason.

5. Memorize Scripture Memory Cards 8 and 9.

Chapter 5

1. What is conversion?
2. Describe your conversion experience.

3. Why did Jesus have to die?
4. Give examples of three different types of conversions in the Bible.
5. Memorize Scripture Memory Card 10.

Chapter 6
1. What is special about the Bible?
2. Name the major sections of the Bible and tell their characteristics.
3. What are some basic tools to use in Bible study?
4. How is the Bible special to you?
5. Memorize Scripture Memory Card 11.

Chapter 7
1. Pretend that God is sitting beside you. Talk to him as you would a close friend.
2. Why should we pray?
3. Read in your Bible the prayer promises: Mark 11:24; Matthew 18:19; John 14:14; Matthew 21:22.
4. What are three basic elements of prayer?
5. Memorize Scripture Memory Card 12.

Chapter 8
1. What is the purpose of the church?
2. Complete the response activity on page 105.
3. You are on a committee to start a new church. What do you want the church to be like? Write your description.
4. Memorize Scripture Memory Card 13.

Chapter 9
1. What is the meaning of baptism?
2. Why do Baptists practice immersion?
3. Match the view of the Lord's Supper with each group.

The Four Historic Views of the Lord's Supper

_____ *a.* Roman Catholics

_____ *b.* Lutherans

_____ *c.* Christians with Calvinist theology

_____ *d.* Christians with Zwinglian theology

(1) The body of Christ is spiritually present in the elements of bread and wine.

(2) The bread and wine actually change to the substance of the flesh and blood of Christ when they are consecrated.

(3) The elements are only symbols used to remind us of Christ's body and blood.

(4) Although the substance of the elements do not change, Christ is bodily present in them.

4. What does the Lord's Supper mean to you?
5. Memorize Scripture Memory Cards 14 and 15.

Chapter 10

1. Define and explain *eschatology.*
2. Contrast the Old and New Testament views of death.
3. What is certain and uncertain about the second coming?
4. What should Christians do to prepare?
5. Memorize Scripture Memory Card 16.

Group Learning Activities

The Group Learning Activities are designed for five sessions of group interaction, using the content of this book. See the Personal Learning Activities for additional ideas.

For each session, each participant will need a book, a Bible, and a pencil. You will need a chalkboard, chalk, and a felt-tip marker.

Session 1: Introduction and Chapter 1

Goal: Participants will examine their concept of God, how God makes himself known, and will focus on the qualities of God described in the writings of John.

Before the Session

• On a large sheet of butcher paper (ceiling to floor length), in large letters vertically write the title of the book. Draw a large *Interrobang* symbol. Place the sheet on a focal wall. (*Double the paper to avoid marking the wall.*) Each session, participants will write on the paper beliefs they can affirm.

- Prepare the following work group assignments:
  Group 1: God Is Spirit
  1. Read John 4:1-42.
  2. Prepare a dramatic sketch of this incident in Jesus' ministry. You will need a narrator, Jesus, and the Samaritan woman.
  3. Be prepared to tell what we know about the nature of God, because he is Spirit. If God is Spirit, then . . . what? See pages 14-16.
  Group 2: God Is Light
  1. Prepare a choral reading, using Scripture passages on God as light. See pages 17-19.
  2. Be prepared to tell how God's light affects our lives.
  Group 3: God Is Love
  1. Paraphrase 1 John 4:7-21.
  2. Be prepared to describe God's love. What adjectives would you use to describe God's love?

During the Session

1. As they arrive, give each participant a book and a pencil. Ask participants to complete the response activity on page 9.

2. When all persons have arrived and have worked on the response activity for at least two to five minutes, state that our belief in God is a basis for all our beliefs. Introduce the study, explaining the meaning of the *Interrobang* symbol as it is described in the Introduction. State that this symbol will be our focus for the study. We will seek to affirm some of our basic beliefs, recognizing that there always will be some unanswered questions.

3. Form pairs. Ask partners to share what they have written regarding their concept of God. (Allow about 2 min.)

4. Ask each pair to join another pair. Assign to each group one of the inadequate concepts of God: *Resident Policeman, Parental Hangover, Grand Old Man, Managing Director*. Ask each group to discuss its concept as described by the author, then to discuss the way people live out that concept (5 to 7 min.). In the large group, briefly review each concept with reports from small groups. State that these concepts aren't all wrong, but they are inadequate.

5. In pairs again, share ways God made himself known (2 min.).

Note ways the author learned about God (pp. 11-14). List on the chalkboard: people, nature, Bible, Jesus. Ask, Does this parallel your experience?

6. State that in this study, we want to become acquainted with the nature of God. The author has used the writings of John for this focus. Regroup in clusters of four to eight. Give to each group one of the group assignments. (Allow 15 to 20 min. for group work.)

7. Call for the report from Group 1. After they have completed their report, a member of the group will write on the butcher paper: *God is Spirit*. After the second and third groups report, they will write their sentence of affirmation on the butcher paper.

8. Encourage participants to memorize Scripture Memory Cards 1-3 as an outgrowth of this session. They may begin working on cards 4-7 in preparation for the next session.

9. Close the session by singing "Great Is Thy Faithfulness," "How Great Thou Art," "He's Everything to Me" (all in *Baptist Hymnal,* 1975), or "God Is So Good" (p. 76, *Sing 'n' Celebrate!* 1971).

Session 2: Chapters 2 and 3

Goal: Participants will affirm that Jesus was truly human and truly divine and that the Holy Spirit is God's presence today.

Before the Session

• Ask four or five persons to role-play the discussion between Jesus and his disciples as recorded in Matthew 16:13-20.

During the Session

1. As people gather, sing several stanzas of the chorus "Jesus in the Morning" (p. 1, *Sing 'n' Celebrate!* 1971). Lead in a prayer for insight and understanding in this study.

2. The role play should then be presented spontaneously. Ask, How do you think Jesus felt about Simon Peter's response?

3. Ask participants to read pages 26-32 to discover why God sent Jesus. After two or three minutes of silence, discuss God's purpose in sending Jesus. Ask someone to write on the butcher paper this affirmation: *In Jesus, God has come to us.*

4. Now we will look at Jesus' birth, life, and death from a divine

and human perspective. Divide into three groups; assign each group one phrase: birth, life, death. Using the book and their Bibles, each group is to show how Jesus was both human and divine during that phase of his life (15 min.).

5. Call for reports in the large group. Then, write on the butcher paper the affirmation: *Jesus was truly human and truly God*.

6. State that when Jesus approached his death, he promised that God would send the Holy Spirit. Because we think of things concretely, we have difficulty understanding a presence which cannot be seen.

Explain the Trinity by comparing it to a person and his relationships:

mother . . . daughter . . . wife

father . . . son . . . husband

Stress the importance of balancing our emphasis in the Trinity.

7. The Holy Spirit is a person. He has qualities of personality. These are expressed in the lives of Christ's followers. Ask participants to turn to the Scrambled Word Puzzle on page 125. Allow individuals five minutes to unscramble the words. Discuss their answers. Write on the butcher paper a statement of affirmation regarding the Holy Spirit: *The Holy Spirit is the person in the Trinity who touches us*.

8. Read aloud Galatians 5:22-25. Pray that the Holy Spirit may produce fruit in the persons participating in this study.

Remind participants to memorize Scripture Memory Cards 8-10 for the next session.

Session 3: Chapters 4 and 5

Goal: Participants will recognize that God created people with freedom of will and that they must make a decision about living in relationship to God.

Before the Session

• On a large strip of paper, write the statement for the debate.

During the Session

1. As participants arrive, give each one a pencil. On the checklist "What Is a Person?" on page 126, they are to check statements with

which they agree. (Allow 5 min.)

Repeat Scripture Memory Card 8.

On the butcher paper write the affirmation: *A person is created by God, in his image.*

2. Read Psalm 8. Speak to the concept of persons being created in the image of God, using the ideas on pages 53-55.

3. Divide into two groups to debate the statement: *Man is essentially evil.* Assign the *pro* side to one team and the *con* side to the other team. Each group will have ten minutes to form its arguments based on the book and biblical references cited. Each group will select a spokesperson.

Call for the debate. Allow each spokesperson two minutes to present his position. After each person has spoken, other team members may speak.

Lead the group to conclusions regarding both good and evil coexisting within a human being. Read Romans 7:14-17,21-23. Repeat in unison Romans 7:22-23 (Scripture Memory Card 9).

4. There is need for continuing cleansing by God. Conversion meets a basic need of every person for help in overcoming evil and living in Christ.

Divide into three groups. Assign to each group one of the following conversion experiences:

- The Ethiopian eunuch (Acts 8:26-39)
- Saul of Tarsus (Acts 9:1-21)
- Philippian Jailer (Acts 16:16-34)

Each group is to present a brief dramatic sketch. Allow five to seven minutes for group work and ten minutes for presentations. Point out the difference in the conversions and the conditions which led to the conversions. Ask, Which of these three is most like your conversion experience?

5. Ask participants to read pages 68-70 to discover what being a Christian means. As you discuss responses, list the following on the chalkboard:

Being a Christian means . . .
- Coming to oneself (repentance)
- Accepting Jesus Christ as Savior

The results are . . .
- A new life

- A new relationship
- A new life-style

6. Ask, Why is conversion necessary? Recall the conversation between Jesus and Nicodemus. Repeat in unison John 3:5-6 (Scripture Memory Card 10). Write on the butcher paper: *Conversion is the process of committing one's life to God's leadership.*

7. With all eyes closed, ask group members to imagine themselves alone with God. Draw a circle around themselves and concentrate only on their communication with him. Ask all to participate as if this were a new experience for each one.

Guide communication with these thoughts: In your private talk with God—

- Admit that you have a need (you are a sinner).
- Ask God to forgive you for sin.
- Invite him to come into your life.
- Tell him you want to follow him in obedience.
- Thank God for his love, for sending his Son to die for you, and for giving you true life.

Close the session by singing "I Have Decided to Follow Jesus" (p. 191, *Baptist Hymnal,* 1975).

Remind participants to memorize Scripture Memory Cards 11 and 12 for the next session.

Session 4: Chapters 6 and 7

Goal: Participants will examine facts about the Bible and prayer, and will recognize the importance of using both as resources for personal Christian growth.

Before the Session

- Prepare a display of a variety of Bibles: old family Bible, King James Version, large print, different translations, a modern version with pictures.
- Provide typing paper (2 sheets per person).
- On a poster or the chalkboard, write the following:

Prayer is . . . only for certain times of the day
talking with God.*
fellowship with God.*

a long speech made to God.

a formal way of communicating with God.

listening to God.*

constant communication with God.*

an attitude of mind.*

Note: Do not put asterisks on the poster. These indicate statements which should be circled during the discussion.

During the Session

1. As participants arrive, ask them to work in twos to review their Scripture Memory Cards (1-10).

2. Call attention to the display of Bibles. Point out the miracle of the preservation of the Bible through the centuries, using information on pages 77-78.

3. Give each person a sheet of paper and a pencil. Ask that each person make a chart of the books of the Bible, grouped as follows.

Old Testament	*New Testament*
Law	Gospels
History	History
Poetry	Paul's Letters
Major Prophets	Pastoral Letters
Minor Prophets	General Epistles
	Apocalypse

After work is completed (5 min.), ask: Why do you think the Bible has this particular arrangement? Why do you think some writings were discarded?

4. Ask someone to write on the butcher paper the affirmation: *The Bible is God's special Word to people.* Repeat in unison 2 Timothy 3:16 (Scripture Memory Card 11).

Discuss the Bible as God's revelation of himself, using the content on pages 75-76.

5. Ask, How can we receive the messages God has for us in the Bible? We must seek to learn what was in the mind of the writer. Discuss the author's suggestions on pages 81-84.

6. State that prayer is another way we can get God's message. In fact, Bible study and prayer go hand in hand in helping us grow as Christians.

Lead each person to draw his own prayer profile (a single line with high points and low points). At what point in life was prayer really important? At what point did God seem especially close? Where are the points of being far away from God and ineffective in praying? Ask for volunteers to share portions of their prayer profiles with the group.

7. Ask participants to indicate which phrases in the definition of prayer (poster or chalkboard) are true. Circle those. On the butcher paper, write the affirmation: *Prayer is communication with God.*

8. Jesus gave us a model for praying in the Lord's Prayer— Matthew 6:9-13. Ask that each person write a personal prayer following the example of Jesus. Distribute paper.

9. In twos, ask participants to pray together using the prayers they have written.

The apostle Paul urged Christians to make prayer an important part of their lives. Repeat in unison 1 Thessalonians 5:16-18 (Scripture Memory Card 12).

The Scripture Memory Cards for Session 5 are 13—16.

Session 5: Chapters 8, 9, and 10

Goal: Participants will better understand the purpose of the church, the observance of baptism and the Lord's Supper, and will look toward the future with hope.

Before the Session
- Obtain pipe cleaners or wire.
- Ask a person to present a pantomime on the life-death-life process of a seed, or draw a chart of the process.

During the Session
1. As participants arrive, give each a piece of wire or a pipe cleaner. Ask participants to form a symbol of what church means to them individually. Allow five minutes for sculpting, then call on individuals to share their work.

2. Write on the butcher paper the affirmation: *A church is a body of believers, banded together to carry out Christ's orders.* As recorded in Matthew 28:18-20, Jesus gave his orders to the disciples and to us today.

Acts 2:42 records the way in which the early church related.

They worshiped together, and they shared their burdens and joys. Repeat in unison Acts 2:42 (Scripture Memory Card 13).

3. Ask, What do the following Scripture verses reveal about the nature of the church?

1 Corinthians 1:23-24 _____

Acts 2:42 _____

Acts 2:45 _____

Acts 5:16 _____

Romans 15:16 _____

Ask participants to read silently the section on why we need the church, pages 101-4. Ask: Do you agree or disagree with the author? Why?

4. Read the following:

Picture yourself in a spaceship traveling to the planet earth in the year A.D. 3000. You are part of a team of historians and archaeologists sent to reconstruct a picture of the civilization of twentieth-century America. Among other things you find the ruins of some buildings, which have one large central room and often a tall tower above it. Frequently in this large, open room you discover two items. One is a big tank which appears capable of holding water. In fact, in some of the rooms over the tank there is a picture of a river with two men standing in it. The second item is a table with the words *In Remembrance of Me* written across it. How would you interpret these facts? What do they tell you about the people who used this room?

The large size of the room: _____

_____

The tank for water: _____

_____

The picture of the river: _____

_____

The table: _____

_____

The inscription on the table: _____

_____

You probably would reach at least one conclusion. The tank and the table somehow represented symbols used in the worship of God. You probably would not be able to go much beyond that unless you were able to find some additional information. The symbols would not mean anything to you. Symbols only have meaning to individuals because they represent an experience.

5. If baptism does not save a person, why do Baptists insist on baptism before church membership? The answer is found in the importance Jesus placed on baptism.

   a. What did Jesus do about baptism? Read Matthew 3:13-17.
   b. What custom did individuals practice when they became followers of Jesus? Read John 4:1-2.
   c. What did Jesus command his disciples to do with new believers? Read Matthew 28:19.

6. Look at baptism as a symbol. Point out the *historic symbols*. How does baptism symbolize salvation through faith in Jesus Christ?

Discuss how baptism is a *personal symbol*. How does baptism symbolize what is happening to the believer in the conversion experience?

As a *public symbol*, how does baptism symbolize the new life of the believer as a part of the Christian church?

On the butcher paper, write: *Baptism is a symbol of our identity with the death, burial, and resurrection of Christ.* Repeat in unison Romans 6:4 (Scripture Memory Card 14).

7. Turn to pages 127-28 and complete the matching exercise on four historic views of the Lord's Supper.

8. Explain how looking backward, looking forward, and looking inward at the Lord's Supper can make it more meaningful.

Repeat in unison 1 Corinthians 11:26 (Scripture Memory Card 15). Write on the butcher paper: *We observe the Lord's Supper as a reminder of what Jesus did for us.*

9. Present the life-death-life process of a seed.

Ask: How does this compare with the life-death-life process of a Christian? How should we face the future? What do we know for certain from the New Testament teachings concerning the second coming of Christ?

Read John 14:1-3. Repeat in unison John 14:3 (Scripture Memory Card 16).

Comment on preparations we should make and attitudes we should have regarding the second coming. Write on the butcher paper: *In the purpose of God, the world is moving toward a fitting conclusion.*

State that the eternal kingdom of God will be ushered in at the second coming of Christ.

10. Call attention to the butcher paper poster. Recall the affirmations of each session. In looking again at the *Interrobang* symbol, remind participants that the study is not complete. There are still questions. The mystery remains. We must continue to learn and grow in our knowledge of God.

Encourage each person who has read the book to notify you. (Send in your church's request for credit, as indicated on p. 143.)

Close the session with a prayer for continued growth and new insights regarding God and his work in the world.

Answers to Scrambled Word Puzzle (p. 125)

a. divine counselor
b. permanent resident
c. personal teacher
d. convinces unbeliever of sin
e. completer of Christ's training
f. personal power
g. boldness in witness

Note: These group activities were compiled by Martha Jo Glazner from the work of Hazel Ruth Bell, Barbara W. Wingate, and Rebecca S. Hayes in *I Believe* and *I Believe, Volume 2.*

Notes

Chapter 1

[1] J. B. Phillips, *Your God Is Too Small* (New York: The Macmillan Company, 1961), p. vi. Used by permission.

[2] This quotation is from the *Good News Bible*, the Bible in Today's English Version. Old Testament: Copyright © American Bible Society 1976; New Testament: Copyright © American Bible Society 1966, 1971, 1976. Used by permission. Subsequent quotations are marked GNB.

[3] From the *New American Standard Bible*. Copyright © The Lockman Foundation, 1960, 1962, 1963, 1971, 1972, 1973, 1975. Used by permission. Subsequent quotations are marked NASB.

[4] Verses marked TLB are taken from *The Living Bible*. Copyright © Tyndale House Publishers, Wheaton, Illinois, 1971. Used by permission. Subsequent quotations are marked TLB.

[5] Reprinted with permission of Macmillan Publishing Co., Inc. from J. B. Phillips: *The New Testament in Modern English*, Revised Edition. © J. B. Phillips, 1958, 1960, 1972. Subsequent quotations are marked Phillips.

[6] From the Revised Standard Version of the Bible, copyrighted 1946, 1952, © 1971, 1973. Subsequent quotations are marked RSV.

Chapter 2

[1] From *The Encyclopedia of Religious Quotations*, edited and compiled by Frank S. Mead (Old Tappan, New Jersey: Fleming H. Revell Company, 1965), p. 49. Used by permission.

[2] James S. Stewart, *The Strong Name* (New York: Charles Scribner's Sons, 1941), p. 78. Used by permission.

[3] Mead, *op. cit.*, p. 60.

Chapter 3

[1] Bernard L. Ramm, *Rapping About the Spirit* (Waco: Word Books, 1974), p. 11.

Chapter 4

[1] From *The Encyclopedia of Religious Quotations*, edited and compiled by Frank S. Mead (Old Tappan, New Jersey: Fleming H. Revell Company, 1965), pp. 288-96. Used by permission.

[2] William Golding, *Lord of the Flies* (New York: Capricorn Books, 1959), p. 192. Used by permission.

[3] *Ibid.*, p. 186.

[4] A. C. Craig, *Preaching in a Scientific Age* (New York: Charles Scribner's Sons, 1954), p. 72. Used by permission.

[5] R. Lofton Hudson, *Helping Each Other Be Human* (Waco: Word Books, 1970), p. 152. Used by permission.

[6] From HOLY BIBLE *New International Version*, copyright © 1978, New York

Bible Society. Used by permission. Subsequent quotations are marked NIV.
⁷Mead, *op. cit.*, p. 292.

Chapter 5
¹R. Lofton Hudson, *Growing a Christian Personality* (Nashville: The Sunday School Board of the Southern Baptist Convention, 1955), p. 11.

Chapter 6
¹From *The Encyclopedia of Religious Quotations*, edited and compiled by Frank S. Mead (Old Tappan, New Jersey: Fleming H. Revell Company, 1965), p. 73. Used by permission.

Chapter 7
¹D. Elton Trueblood, *A Place to Stand* (New York: Harper and Row, 1969), p. 100. Used by permission.

Chapter 8
¹From *The Encyclopedia of Religious Quotations*, edited and compiled by Frank S. Mead (Old Tappan, New Jersey: Fleming H. Revell Company, 1965), p. 75. Used by permission.
²William Barclay, *The Letter to the Hebrews* (Philadelphia: The Westminster Press, 1955), p. 137.
³Mead, *op. cit.*, p. 75.

The Church Study Course

The Church Study Course consists of a variety of short-term credit courses for adults and youth and noncredit foundational units for children and preschoolers.

Study course materials are flexible enough to be adapted to the needs of any Baptist church. The resources are published in several different formats—textbooks of various sizes, workbooks, and kits.

Adults and youth can earn study course credit through individual or group study.

This book is the text for Youth Course 3376 of the subject area Baptist Doctrine.

This course is designed for five hours of group study. Credit is awarded for attending class sessions and reading the book. A person who is absent for one or more sessions must complete the "Personal Learning Activities" for the material missed. A person desiring credit for individual study should read the book and complete the "Personal Learning Activities."

After the course is completed, the teacher, the study course clerk, or any person designated by the church should complete Form 151 (Church Study Course Credit Request, Revised 1975), and send it to the Awards Office, 127 Ninth Avenue, North, Nashville, Tennessee 37234. Individuals also may request credit by mailing the form to the Awards Office.

Credit for this study may be applied to one or more diplomas in the Church Study Course.

Other Doctrine Books for Youth

Youth Affirm: The Doctrine of God by Dan G. Kent
Youth Affirm: The Doctrine of Man by Paul D. Brewer
Youth Affirm: The Doctrine of Salvation by Lavonn D. Brown
Youth Affirm: The Doctrine of Missions by Ed Seabough and
    Bill O'Brien
Youth Affirm: The Doctrine of the Church by Jimmy Allen

All available from the Baptist Book Store nearest you.

Cut along this line

INSTRUCTIONS: If requested by the teacher, fill in this form and give it to him when the course is completed. If preferred, mail this request for course credit to

AWARDS OFFICE
THE SUNDAY SCHOOL BOARD, SBC
127 NINTH AVENUE, NORTH
NASHVILLE, TENNESSEE 37234

State Convention	Association	Indicate Type of Study (X)		Educational
		Class ☐ Individual ☐	Lesson Course ☐	Institution ☐

CHURCH

Church Name

Mailing Address

City, State, Zip Code

MAIL TO

Mail to (If Different from Church Address)

Street, Route, or P.O. Box

City, State, Zip Code

3376

LAST NAME	FIRST NAME AND MIDDLE INITIAL	MRS. (X)	COURSE TITLE
			Truths That Make a Difference